"Alvin Sanders is a leader wl _____ _ry story of his life and ministry. ___ _____ and focus on the gospel at work in urban communities and communities experiencing the effects of poverty and injustice have translated into a book that will be inspirational and challenging to those who are willing to muster the courage to respond to what they read. Perhaps most importantly, Sanders connects the presence of the local church—enacting the gospel on the sidewalks and intersections of neighborhood life—to the possibility of experiencing something of a common good in our time. I appreciate the narrative focus; stories that weave throughout the wisdom Alvin has left for us to learn from as we read. It reinforces the credibility those of us who know Alvin can observe, even from afar, and provides a context to the insights he shares. *Uncommon Church* resists the temptation to cave to an overly spiritualized vision of the kingdom that sees no compulsion to deal with the injustice of the world while still maintaining a vibrant and nourishing spiritual center that comes from his many years of pastoral experience. We all would do well to read it, share it widely, and then get to work living out the wisdom we find."

Adam Gustine, author of *Becoming a Just Church: Cultivating Communities of God's Shalom,* and assistant director, Center for Social Concerns, University of Notre Dame

"The message of *Uncommon Church* is clear and simple: the fundamental way that God means to heal and transform impoverished communities is through the presence and loving witness of healthy churches. That argument, however, hinges on an understanding of what it means to be the church that lies beyond many of our assumptions and dominant paradigms. Grounded in keen biblical insights, supported by practical strategies born out of experiential wisdom, and replete with stories that are as instructive as they are inspiring, this is a must-have book for anyone desiring to join God's church-based agenda for healing the brokenness and combating the evil and injustices of our world, especially as they are manifest in the hood."

JR Rozko, national director, Missio Alliance

"Alvin Sanders's book shines a spotlight on the power of the local church to transform whole communities when the gospel is lived out in our neighborhoods. At a time when many are predicting the demise of the church in America, *Uncommon Church* charts a path forward that leads to deep and lasting transformation for individuals and whole communities. This book is deeply theological, refreshingly practical, and needs to be read by every church leader."

Jeannette Cochran, executive pastor of Seneca Creek Community Church, Gaithersburg, Maryland

"*Uncommon Church* is a must-read for anyone who senses God's call to do ministry in an underresourced community. I'm convinced that healthy churches working for the common good of their communities for the glory of God are an indispensable ingredient to seeing underresourced communities thrive."

Philip Abode, lead pastor of Crossover Bible Church, Tulsa, Oklahoma

"Alvin's extensive experience and expertise in leading churches toward engaging in effective community transformation shines through in this work. He takes complex principles, tensions, and best practices and communicates them in accessible and practical ways. If you are seeking to see the church live out a transforming presence within communities of material poverty, you will find this book to be an essential tool. I am eager to get this book into the hands of every leader within the ministry I serve."

Ruth Evans, executive director, Unite Network

"In *Uncommon Church*, Dr. Alvin Sanders combines his three decades of experience planting, pastoring, and empowering urban churches with his academic expertise to argue for a new approach to starting and maintaining local congregations. Sanders calls for churches to stop seeing 'certain people' as projects but instead recognize their full humanity and role as fellow believers in the body of Christ. In the midst of societal crossroads when many are questioning the role of the local congregation, Sanders offers a key perspective on how the church can live out its mission by supporting its neighbors and fighting for justice for all."

Junia Howell, assistant professor of sociology, University of Pittsburgh

"Alvin Sanders has a heart for the urban poor and a passion for the church. He has planted and pastored a church in the heart of a community of urban poverty, trained and mentored urban ministry leaders, and now leads a ministry that is empowering urban leaders and partnering with local churches to reach their communities with the gospel. In his book *Uncommon Church*, he draws on the truth of the Scriptures and his personal experience to challenge local churches to be the foundation from which God's people can pursue the common good in communities. His focus on personal holiness and justice along with declaring and demonstrating the gospel is both refreshing and powerful. If you love the local church and want to make an eternal difference in your community, his message is one you need to hear and put into practice."

Kevin Kompelien, president of the Evangelical Free Church of America

"Awake to the needs of the urban poor, Americans are ready to embrace solutions. With faith, wisdom, and experience, Alvin Sanders has one to offer: the healthy church in the hood. This book is everything that practical Christian theology ought to be: grounded in theology, clear-eyed about the real world, focused on godly outcomes, and expressed in plain language. There's not a shred of nonsense in this book: no false pieties, no simplistic formulas, no sugarcoating what is inevitably an unremitting struggle. But there is a truckload of hope on every page. Here is an agenda for an American church that may have lost its way but dare not lose its hope. And here is a rejoinder to those who would try again (and fail again) to 'fix' the hood with anything less than the power of God."

Jon Weatherly, provost of Johnson University

"The voices are many these days—some loud, some soft, some angry, some confused, and some silent and afraid to speak. *Uncommon Church* is written for these times. It is full of grace and guidance to all the voices, synthesizing the answers within the power of the local church. Every pastor and aspiring pastor should read this book! It will bring inspiration, information, and opportunity for the Spirit to move, unlocking the potential in the local church. The results will be exponential in healing and empowering communities for the common good."

Jo Anne Lyon, general superintendent emerita, the Wesleyan Church

"Alvin Sanders provides a way forward for those desiring to bring social justice and spiritual conversion together in their local church. This is a challenging and practical resource for those engaged in urban church work. Alvin's vision should also capture the imagination of the rest of the church. How might a generous church help without hurting? How might the American church marry charity and witness? Alvin leads the way. Do not read this alone; invite your team along on the journey."

Tyler McKenzie, lead pastor of Northeast Christian Church, Louisville, Kentucky

"*Uncommon Church* paints a vision and provides a roadmap for revival in America's urban centers. Alvin Sanders is a practitioner of this work, so his approach is proven and not just theory. This is a must-read for every leader with a heart for the poor and a desire to see revival in your community!"

Chuck Mingo, Oakley campus pastor, Crossroads Church/Cincinnati

"*Uncommon Church* is an uncommon book that integrates passion for social justice with Christ-centered spirituality. Dr. Sanders has produced a readable primer on urban ministry that weds community development with the development of healthy, disciple-making churches."

Craig Ott, professor of mission and intercultural studies at Trinity Evangelical Divinity School

"It is critical that the body of Christ supports, resources, and equips healthy local churches within urban poor communities. Alvin writes with decades of both theological reflection and practical experience in community development and local church leadership. This book is an important tool for cultivating vision and strengthening leaders to do the important work of church ministry in urban poor communities."

Dennae Pierre, codirector of City to City North America

"Alvin Sanders in *Uncommon Church* asks that we take seriously the common good of all God's people, both in a big-picture way—by engaging with the systems—and in the mustard seed way—by tangibly loving our neighbor as ourselves. Still as revolutionary, as uncommon today as it was back in the day of Jesus. *Uncommon Church* gives us inspiring examples from a hope-filled modern prophet."

Laura Sumner Truax, senior pastor of LaSalle Street Church, Chicago

UNCOMMON

CHURCH

COMMUNITY
TRANSFORMATION
FOR THE
COMMON GOOD

ALVIN SANDERS

FOREWORD BY EFREM SMITH

An imprint of InterVarsity Press
Downers Grove, Illinois

InterVarsity Press
P.O. Box 1400, Downers Grove, IL 60515-1426
ivpress.com
email@ivpress.com

InterVarsity Press® is the book-publishing division of InterVarsity Christian Fellowship/USA®, a movement of students and faculty active on campus at hundreds of universities, colleges, and schools of nursing in the United States of America, and a member movement of the International Fellowship of Evangelical Students. For information about local and regional activities, visit intervarsity.org.

All Scripture quotations, unless otherwise indicated, are taken from The Holy Bible, New International Version®, NIV®. Copyright © 1973, 1978, 1984, 2011 by Biblica, Inc.™ Used by permission of Zondervan. All rights reserved worldwide. www.zondervan.com. The "NIV" and "New International Version" are trademarks registered in the United States Patent and Trademark Office by Biblica, Inc.™

While any stories in this book are true, some names and identifying information may have been changed to protect the privacy of individuals.

Cover design and image composite: Faceout Studio
Interior design: Jeanna Wiggins
Image: old Manhattan building: © Busà Photography / Moment Collection / Getty Images

ISBN 978-0-8308-4162-2 (print)
ISBN 978-0-8308-4163-9 (digital)

Printed in the United States of America ∞

InterVarsity Press is committed to ecological stewardship and to the conservation of natural resources in all our operations. This book was printed using sustainably sourced paper.

Library of Congress Cataloging-in-Publication Data
A catalog record for this book is available from the Library of Congress.

P	25	24	23	22	21	20	19	18	17	16	15	14	13	12	11	10	9	8	7	6	5	4	3	2	1
Y	37	36	35	34	33	32	31	30	29	28	27	26	25	24	23	22	21	20							

THIS BOOK IS DEDICATED TO
THE PEOPLE OF GOD WHO BELIEVE IN
THE POWER OF THE LOCAL CHURCH
WITHIN COMMUNITIES OF POVERTY.

"But we do not belong to those
who shrink back and are destroyed,
but to those who have faith and are saved."

(HEBREWS 10:39)

CONTENTS

Foreword by Efrem Smith 1

PART 1: UNCOMMON CHURCH

1 Advocacy Is Not Enough 7

2 What Would Jesus Do? 20
Poverty Is a Condition, Not an Identity

3 Jesus Did, Not Jesus Would 37
Jesus and the Condition of Poverty

4 The People of God 53
God's Plan for a Broken World

5 Doing Healthy Church 69
Seven Habits Toward Spiritual Maturity

PART 2: SEEKING THE COMMON GOOD

6 Faith *and* Works 91
Eliminating the Tension Between
Evangelism and Justice

7 There Goes the Neighborhood 108
Understanding the Powers That Be

8 Championing the Community 126
Empowering Grassroots Leaders and Workers

9 Chasing Wild Dreams 142
Examples of Faith, Hope, and Love in Action

10 The Kingdom Is in Us 151

Acknowledgments 155

Notes 157

FOREWORD

EFREM SMITH

T HE CHURCH has had an interesting relationship with the cities of the United States of America. A segment of the church abandoned cities during the racial integration of the 1960s and '70s. In many ways the suburban megachurches of today are built off the backs of white flight followed by the flight of families of color with the ability to escape the black and brown cities and underresourced ghettos. At the same time, cities have been the object of the urban missionaries of the 1970s and '80s who left evangelical college campuses with a passion to evangelize the urban poor. They came with Bible clubs, Christian education, and one-to-one relational evangelism supplemented by gospel tracts.

The city has also been the church planting and revitalization ground of many African American and multiethnic churches over the years. I am actually a product of these urban church models. The buildings that were abandoned by the white churches that fled were filled with new African American and multiethnic churches in the 1980s and '90s. Church buildings originally built by American Baptists, Southern Baptists, Presbyterians, and

Lutherans were now occupied by black denominationally rooted congregations such as the Church of God in Christ, the National Baptist Convention USA, the Progressive National Baptist Convention, and the African Methodist Episcopal Church. These churches represent expressions of the storefront church, community-engaging church, and megachurch models. Multiethnic church plants have become a recent trend in the city from the 1990s up until the present moment. These churches are in demand because of the increasing multiethnic and multicultural diversity of the city.

The city is also the place where the church is dying. One might argue that there is no more need for new churches in the cities of the United States of America because some communities have multiple churches on the same block. But if you attend a number of these churches on any given Sunday, you find congregations that are on life support with no current strategy for thriving and flourishing in its surrounding mission field. The city is both a birthing center and a cemetery for the church.

And yet the city is expanding. We are living in not only an ever-increasing multiethnic reality in the United States but also one of urbanization. What is urban continues to expand. Suburbs are looking more like cities and rural areas more like suburbs. Gentrification within cities is revealing a reverse migration of the highly educated and upper middle class returning to the midtown and uptown communities of the city. This offers new missional opportunities for the church. The whole church on some level is going to have to function as a multiethnic and urban church.

The church must also continue to be mindful of the most vulnerable among us. Compassion, mercy, justice, and reconciliation are just as much biblical mandates as evangelism and discipleship. As a matter of biblical fact, there are actually more references in

Scripture regarding justice than discipleship, though I would never downplay the importance of discipleship. The Bible doesn't simply present the poor and vulnerable as objects of pity, but as the receivers of healing, liberation, empowerment, and authority. This narrative and missional venture is why this book is so important.

Alvin Sanders has spent years as an urban church planter, public theologian, denominational executive, and urban missions leader. He has a deep passion for the church, racial reconciliation, and the empowerment of indigenous urban leaders. This book provides transformative insights for a church that can serve as a force for kingdom advancement in the city. Allow this resource to challenge you, change you, and equip you so that you might serve God's mission for our cities.

PART 1
UNCOMMON CHURCH

1

ADVOCACY IS NOT ENOUGH

Show me a hero, and I'll write you a tragedy.

F. SCOTT FITZGERALD

Show Me a Hero by Lisa Belkin highlights a low-income housing fight in Yonkers, New York, during the 1980s not unlike conflicts that continue to happen throughout the nation. Yonkers, like many cities, was racially segregated, and the National Association for the Advancement of Colored People (NAACP) and the federal government teamed up to try to bring change. Together they filed a lawsuit against Yonkers with the goal of integrating the city's institutions, such as the housing system, and they won a court order that the city desegregate.

Yonkers had followed the pattern of many cities, limiting public housing to a small section of the city, resulting in the isolation of its poor residents. Those who benefited from this illegal practice decided not to let four decades of segregation go quietly into the night; they fought the court order fiercely. When the inevitable happened and low-income housing was built on the historically white side of town, ugliness ensued, reminiscent of the civil rights clashes of the 1960s.

The hero of this story is the young mayor, Nick Wasicsko, who at twenty-eight became a rising star when he unexpectedly won the mayoral race in the middle of the conflict. The campaign promise that swept him to victory was his pledge to appeal the desegregation order. When he came into office in 1987, promising to fight the housing mandate, he realized there was no way to keep his campaign promise, and he became an advocate of integrated housing. The decision was somewhere between a political expediency—the city budget was going to crash if he didn't go along with the order—and an authentic change of heart.

Predictably, there were dire consequences. Wasicsko was bullied and threatened, and he was eventually voted out. He bounced back and returned as a councilman in the 1990s, but he killed himself in 1993 at the age of thirty-four.

Is advocacy a vicious cycle that dooms a person in the end? It certainly can seem that way. In 2020 we're *still* fighting battles concerning fair housing. As people of God who have an eternal perspective, we definitely should play a role in helping to solve justice issues such as these.

You may not have heard the name Howard Thurman before, yet if you haven't, I would bet you unknowingly know of his work. He was called Dr. Martin Luther King Jr.'s personal theologian, as Dr. King based much of his work in Thurman's teachings. Thurman's most famous work was a book titled *Jesus and the Disinherited.* If you have never read it, I highly encourage you to do so.

Oftentimes this work is situated in liberation theology, yet I don't agree. Although we can sift elements of that genre from its pages, I would categorize his insights more in the realm of providing a spirituality that is liberating. He says repeatedly in the book that he is exploring "what the teachings of Jesus have to say to those who stand at a moment in history with their backs against the wall . . . the poor, the disinherited, the dispossessed."

In other words, he imagined how people on the margins of society could remain human despite the "three hounds of hell that track the trail of the disinherited"—fear, hypocrisy, and hatred. His advice was to abandon the pursuit of these things as answers to their situation and honor God. In the chapter titled "Jesus—An Interpretation" he frames holiness as the key to survival:

> In the midst of this psychological climate Jesus began his teaching and his ministry. His words were directed to the House of Israel, a minority within the Greco-Roman world, smarting under the loss of status, freedom, and autonomy, haunted by the dream of the restoration of a lost glory and a former greatness. His message focused on the urgency of a radical change in the inner attitude of the people. . . . Again and again he came back to the inner life of the individual. With increasing insight and startling accuracy he placed his finger on the "inward center" as the crucial arena where the issues would determine the destiny of his people.[1]

Thurman clearly believed that a mindset followed by behaviors that demonstrated being people of God was critical. However, there is more to the story. If we look at the original 1935 essay "Good News for the Underprivileged" on which the book was based, he makes it clear that the disinherited being the people of God goes beyond just personal salvation. He stresses a transformation of society in order to move to a new day where the oppression ends.

THE CHURCH NEEDS WILLING WORKERS

I hope to stand on the shoulders of Thurman. This book is for people who believe in the power of the local church to make a difference in the lives of the urban poor. Many who fight for justice for the poor come from Christian backgrounds. However, the American church has two main problems when it comes to addressing justice for the poor. The first is philosophical: too many Christians treat the poor as charitable goodwill projects instead of as people among whom the church can be God's witnesses. Charity and witness are not mutually exclusive.

Poverty is a condition people live in that needs to be addressed from a godly perspective. In this book, we'll engage hard truths about poor neighborhoods and explore pathways to ministry in those places.

Christ said, "I will build my church" (Matthew 16:18). He didn't say he would build a food pantry, a tutoring program, or a community development enterprise. He added, "And the gates of Hades will not overcome it." I am all for good works, but I believe the witness of the church is an undervalued and overlooked asset when it comes to urban poverty.

A healthy church is a holy place, because holiness lies at the heart of the Christian faith. The apostle Peter wrote, "It is written, 'Be holy, because I am holy'" (1 Peter 1:16). We're instructed to be like God—holy in everything we do. Holiness displays the character of God; it means being set apart for service to God. As we do this, we have the privilege of influencing situations for God's glory. A key understanding that many miss when ministering to those who are marginalized is that *holiness is the way to victory.*

Many mistakenly think that the pursuit of holiness happens only on a personal level. But the church is also to pursue holiness socially through God-created institutions. This is where advocacy comes in. Social institutions are permanent and complicated structures formed to meet basic human needs. They are powerful, they endure for generations, and they influence many lives. The church is one of those institutions, sociologically speaking. Pursuing holiness on the institutional level means seeking the common good of a community.

What is *the common good*? It is the answer to two questions. What do those who have put their faith in Christ have in common with those who have not? And what can the local church do to make the world a better place for them? The local church ought to understand differences and act on commonalities. God wants all neighborhoods to flourish, and they can't if institutions don't function well.

The second problem—closely related to the first—is theological. Or more accurately, I should say a lack thereof. What I am about to write may trigger a "Boomer alert" moment, but hear me out. Besides, I am not of the Boomer generation but of Gen X—you know, the generation no one cares about! The point is I am old enough to detect a subtle shift.

When I started off in urban ministry in 1991, I believe a huge problem was many had good theology but didn't live it out well among the urban poor. I've noticed we've come full circle. Today I see people doing a lot of advocacy in and for poor neighborhoods, but their actions have little to no theology behind them. When this is the case, the local church becomes an afterthought. If we say we are Christian, this cannot be. There is no way around the fact that the Bible makes it clear: the local church is the hope of the world, regardless of where it is located. I'll state my case for this later in the book.

UNDERSTANDING THE HOOD

When academicians study institutional dysfunction, they flock to the hood. A hood, as I define it, is a place where a large percentage of the residents have inadequate financial resources. Traditionally the word *hood* referred to certain inner-city neighborhoods, but in today's gentrifying world, a hood can also be in a suburb. Ironically the challenges in these neighborhoods mirror those in rural areas.

Hoods don't just happen. Policies and practices make it tough for groups of people to leave their neighborhoods and/or to make them better. These policies and practices grow out of underlying issues of race and class. The sociological term for this is *racialization.*

A racialized society is a society wherein race matters profoundly for differences in life experiences, life opportunities, and social relationships. It is one that allocates different economic, political, social, and psychological rewards to groups along racial lines.[2] Typically when whites move out of a neighborhood at a high rate, so does access to financial resources and a good quality of life. The neighborhood is doomed to fail, mainly because it isn't given a fair shake. The mostly black and brown people left behind are seen as projects rather than as people. And the prevailing thought is that if they would get their act together, they could escape that hellhole. People drive through such neighborhoods as quickly as possible, and they certainly don't want to be caught there at night. Hoods are city or suburban quarantine areas for high poverty.

In April 2001 Timothy Thomas, a nineteen-year-old African American with a history of nonviolent misdemeanors, was shot and killed by a Cincinnati police officer. It was Ferguson *before* Ferguson. His death caused outrage, riots, and civil disobedience, resulting in millions of dollars of damage.[3] In the middle of it all, right in the Over-the-Rhine neighborhood, where the shooting occurred, my wife and I planted a church called River of Life. At that time, Over-the-Rhine was the second most violent neighborhood in the country.

I no longer serve as pastor of River of Life, and two decades later the church has become a beacon of hope, exhibiting what God can do when people from all walks work together for the advancement of the kingdom in the hood.

I share this snapshot for your assurance. In 2013 I wrote a personal mission statement that I have structured my life around: I have been put on this earth to chase hard after God, love my family, and invest in those who invest in the poor. I wrote this book as a small part of living out my personal mission. I live that personal mission out in my current position as president/CEO of World Impact. World Impact empowers urban leaders and partners with local churches to reach their cities with the gospel. We are committed to bringing hope to the hood. Our dream is a healthy church for every impoverished community.

THE UNCOMMON CHURCH MODEL

I'm often asked, "What's the biggest need of impoverished neighborhoods?"

I reply, "Healthy local churches."

"Not food, clothing, or housing?"

"No, none of those."

My experience is that when healthy churches exist in the hood, they become major players advocating for raising the quality of life there, which includes things like food, clothing, and housing. And due to the challenges, we can never have enough church leaders and workers.

In my three decades of urban ministry, I've seen the following story play out countless times: A person goes in to do good works in the hood. Time passes, and he or she gets frustrated because the residents don't "act right"—that is, upper-middle-class standards aren't met in response to the help given. The

relationship goes sideways, and all involved are embittered by
the experience. Contrast that with how suburban populations
are treated. They are rarely viewed as objects, and personhood
is automatically granted to them; no deficit must be overcome
to be considered a person.

To do good works, we must support the common good of the
community. The goal is to build enough goodwill to form healthy
relationships and to share the gospel, leading to the assimilation
of people into a church. That's always the finish line in suburban
contexts, yet rarely is it the finish line in the hood. Good works,
advocacy, and goodwill are helpful; but what about the good news
of the gospel?

There's nothing easy about doing church in the hood, and advocacy driven by a biblically based desire to demonstrate God's
love is needed to transform lives and communities. Some disagree
with mixing the social sciences with theology due to a concern
that secular social science knowledge will override proper biblical
knowledge. But I don't think the Bible divides the revelation of
knowledge into either/or categories. Scripture makes it clear that
all truthful knowledge comes from God.

The social sciences (sociology, psychology, and so on) are av-
enues for studying God's general revelation of creation. The
mountains we see, the amazing bodies we possess, and science
itself are all evidence of a creator. This type of revelation is
available to everyone, regardless of whether they believe in God
or not. God's gift to all human beings is the ability to wake up and
realize through nature, history, and human experience that there
is something bigger than them operating in this world. The apostle
Paul wrote, "For since the creation of the world God's invisible
qualities—his eternal power and divine nature—have been
clearly seen, being understood from what has been made, so that

people are without excuse" (Romans 1:20). Special revelation is the knowledge gained through the study of God through the Scriptures (theology).

Continuously improving our knowledge of the special revelation of God (the Bible) should be a key part of our lives. Paul stated that as his goal when he wrote, "I want to know Christ—yes, to know the power of his resurrection and participation in his sufferings, becoming like him in his death" (Philippians 3:10). I would hope this is the goal of every believer.

A biblical worldview acknowledges that all truth comes from God, so there should be no conflict between good theology and truthful social science. In any Sociology 101 class, we learn that five institutions serve as the building blocks of any society:

+ family—the space to procreate and pass along values, attitudes, and beliefs about life

+ government—a system to preserve order, which takes the form of formal or informal laws, punishments, provision for those in need, etc.

+ education—skill-set development for becoming a productive a member of whatever society one belongs to

+ economics—the production, consumption, and distribution of material goods and services

+ religion (spirituality)—ways to answer the unanswerable, involving moral questions and life purpose, such as who I am, why I exist, and how I treat others

God put these five building blocks into place through general revelation. Therefore societies expect religious institutions to have a response to the challenges they face. What are the challenges faced by the hood? Regardless of whether the hood is in New York or Nairobi, I believe they all share concerns about the following:

+ economic development
+ public safety
+ financial resources
+ infrastructure
+ education
+ housing
+ environment
+ demographics
+ technology
+ health care

The church in the hood must construct itself to be able to address these concerns. It must be a neighborhood anchor. It can do so by playing three critical roles, as shown in figure 1.

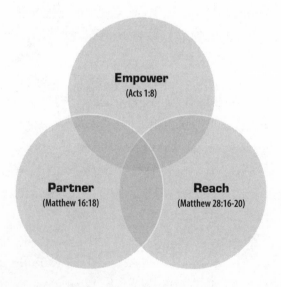

Figure 1. The church's roles in the hood

Empower. "But you will receive power when the Holy Spirit comes on you; and you will be my witnesses in Jerusalem, and in all Judea and Samaria, and to the ends of the earth" (Acts 1:8). God made Jesus king over all creation. Jesus' last act on earth was to give us the Holy Spirit to empower us. We are to go and do *whatever* needs to be done *wherever* it needs to be done. As we go, Jesus promises to be with us.

I know of nothing more empowering than making disciples. To empower someone is to help them do something. Who doesn't need help navigating life? When people think about the hood, they greatly undervalue discipleship. I'm not talking about a need for a vibrant small-group program. If the program is any good, it's just an excuse to disciple people. I'm talking about authentic relationships built over long periods. A healthy local congregation provides space for people to do life together in order to transcend the conditions they're in.

Partner. "And I tell you that you are Peter, and on this rock I will build my church, and the gates of Hades will not overcome it. I will give you the keys of the kingdom of heaven; whatever you bind on earth will be bound in heaven, and whatever you loose on earth will be loosed in heaven" (Matthew 16:18-19). Jesus made a remarkable statement here: one day Peter would be a leader in the church—based on his revelation that Jesus is Lord. Peter never forgot this, as he later wrote that Christ is the chief cornerstone and the church is to be a holy priesthood (1 Peter 2:4-6). He then went on to explain how the church should behave in difficult times.

It's clear that the church is expected to be engaged in the world around it. It can't be silent, as the hood doesn't just need something good to happen; it needs transformation. Through partnership, the local church plays a key role. Because of the way hoods are formed, the community must be built from the inside out. When a congregation becomes an institutional partner with local businesses, schools, and so on, it becomes a church with no walls and a transformative influencer.

Reach. The church looks beyond itself to reach others.

> Then the eleven disciples went to Galilee, to the mountain where Jesus had told them to go. When they saw him, they worshiped him; but some doubted. Then Jesus came to them and said, "All authority in heaven and on earth has been given to me. Therefore go and make disciples of all nations, baptizing them in the name of the Father and of the Son and of the Holy Spirit, and teaching them to obey everything I have commanded you. And surely I am with you always, to the very end of the age." (Matthew 28:16-20)

The church is to seek the common good of the neighborhood by being a compassion and justice center. Reaching the hood is two sides of one coin. *Evangelism* (transmission of the gospel message of the transformative power of following Christ) is the local church's response on a personal level to issues of hood life. *Justice* (genuine pursuit for both peace among and respect toward individuals and people groups) is the local church's contribution to the common good. Both, not one or the other, are needed.

AN OVERVIEW OF *UNCOMMON CHURCH*

This book lays out how to implement an uncommon church model. The first section focuses on what it means to be an uncommon church. I start by examining the wrong question: "What would Jesus do?" It's wrong for two reasons: first, it makes the circumstances front and center instead of what God *said* about the circumstances, and second, Jesus already told us what he did, which is the focus of chapter three. It's a brief look at how Christ approached the condition of poverty. Our job is to learn, obey, and act upon his teaching.

Chapter four traces the special nature of the people of God, from the Garden of Eden to the formation of the church. In the Bible, the people of God have always been identified as those who are in God's empowering presence. In chapter five, I give some practical guidance on how to build a healthy congregation. This model has been tested all over the globe and is successful because it follows closely the model presented in the New Testament. It's also the blueprint I used when I church planted and pastored in the hood.

In part two, we transition toward what it means to work for the common good of the community. Chapter six addresses the unnecessary tension between evangelism and justice. Both are biblical concepts that work in unison. Chapter seven delves into some basics of how hoods were formed. Some hard truths are told, and the Bible teaches that the truth shall set us free. Chapter eight explores the philosophy of the Christian Community Development Association (CCDA), which was founded by John Perkins. It's the template of how a local church can do advocacy for the common good in poor neighborhoods. Chapter nine provides a few stories of people who are doing uncommon church. And in chapter ten you'll find my concluding comments.

One final word: don't expect to find all the answers to your questions in this book, as that's impossible. My goal is to be a guide on the side instead of a sage on a stage. I'm passing along the lessons the Lord has taught me; this book holds just one man's opinion. What I present is *a* model, not *the* model.

I liken this book to a coat. Try it on, and if it fits, it's yours. If it doesn't, take it off! My hope is that it will help you on your learning journey. God be with you as you work to transform your hood.

2

WHAT WOULD JESUS DO?

POVERTY IS A CONDITION, NOT AN IDENTITY

I HATE THE QUESTION What would Jesus do?

Before explaining why, let me apologize if I've offended you. Many have used this question to discern answers to tough decisions, have worn the bracelet, and have decorated their car with the bumper sticker. It's a very popular phrase, yet most of us don't have a clue where it came from. Let's start there.

In the 1890s, Pastor Charles Monroe Sheldon had an idea that he thought would attract people to his church. In his Sunday-night sermons, he told stories of people in dramatic situations grappling with the question What would Jesus do? The sermons ended with cliffhangers, so the listeners had to return the following week to find out what happened. The crowd loved it, and eventually his stories were gathered into a book entitled *In His Steps*. There are not many books people talk about a century later, but this is one of them.

The book became a pop-culture sensation, gaining a worldwide audience. It's estimated to have made as much as thirty million dollars since its release. Its appeal lies in its dramatic spiritual-growth stories. The main characters are members of a wealthy congregation who make a covenant to ask in their daily lives, What would Jesus do? Each of them has a rude awakening.

In the book, the pivotal character is the fictional Pastor Henry Maxwell. He may be a pastor, but he is not a good guy; he's self-centered. Then he starts asking What would Jesus do? in his daily decision-making. He ends up on a spiritual pilgrimage that leads him to the hood, and he decides to tackle tough societal issues. He testifies to his congregation about the change of character he experiences, and that deeply affects how they start living their lives.

His congregation is no ordinary one. It's made up of the town's movers and shakers. For example, a newspaperman tries to run the paper like Jesus would. An heiress wonders what Jesus would do with a million dollars. An author struggles with how to use his writing talent. A playboy socialite wonders if he's spending his time as Jesus would. A singer wrestles with how to best use her gift. One man even has a Job-like experience, losing everything he has because he asked the question.

When you read the book, you resonate with each character. They all are stretched spiritually. So you might be wondering why I have a problem with What would Jesus do? Don't we all want to make the decisions Jesus would make? What's wrong with framing our lives like that? I'm glad you asked.

IT'S ALL ABOUT ME

Here's the dirty little secret behind why many people get involved in urban ministry: we view people in poverty as goodwill projects that will allow us to fulfill our life purpose. It makes us feel good to go down to the hood and "save" somebody. Want to feel like a million bucks? Go serve a turkey dinner to someone down on her luck, witness to and pray for her, and go back home to comfort. Want to raise a million bucks? Show media images showing a community outsider being the hero of the hood.

When I was pastoring, a colleague who worked at another ministry in our community dropped by to talk. I could see she was dejected. She had a heart for the hood and felt that God had called her to change lives. She had left corporate America, taking a massive pay cut.

But she was starting to become bitter because she felt God had abandoned her. Because of the pay cut, she was in as bad financial straits as the people she worked among. Her heart's desire was to help the people, but she felt they were using her. When she started, she had been filled with energy. Now she hated to show up at her office because she feared what the day would bring. Her big dream was crumbling right before her eyes.

She seems to be someone who would ask, What would Jesus do? and then move accordingly. But that question makes the questioner the standard for making moral decisions. The correct answer depends completely on how good a theologian the questioner is; it assumes that the person knows the heart and mind of God. Too many times, people think they know what Jesus would do, so they run to help the hood without *any* practical theology of the poor.

For me, What would Jesus do? often reflects a *savior syndrome*. Typically, people have good intentions and come in to help. They believe either consciously or subconsciously that they will be the ones to save the community. But that's impossible, and my colleague was beginning to realize it.

Let me confess that I am one who has recovered from the savior syndrome. While at a state university, I was studying to become a physical therapist. About halfway through, I realized I didn't want to do that as a career. That's because I served as a volunteer in the hood, where I got tired of seeing impossible situations and wanted desperately to make a difference. I transferred to Bible college, graduated, and promptly embedded myself in an underresourced community. It didn't take long for me to reach the place my colleague was in: embittered and sad.

Being a survivor of savior syndrome, I spent significant time helping her unpack her mindset. And I told her my testimony. Those who are serious about the hood at some point realize there's nothing in it for them except spiritual growth. You end up growing in your faith, abandoning it, or burning out. Freedom is realizing you can't save the hood—only Jesus can.

WHY ARE THEY POOR?

My first full-time ministry position was during the welfare reform era of the 1990s, and my job was to connect families in poverty from social service agencies with churches who were willing to help them go from "welfare to work." Part of the process was to provide training for church members on what to expect.[1]

Like clockwork, there would always be a point in the training when a rant would happen from at least one of the attendees. All rants shared the same premise. They blamed the poor for their plight, ignored counterarguments, and claimed moral superiority. Certainly one of the causes of poverty is unwise moral choices. But it is not the only cause.

There are two prevailing schools of thought regarding the causes of poverty. The first school includes those who believe in the existence of a *culture of poverty*. *Culture* includes the values, attitudes, and beliefs people hold. Culture-of-poverty advocates believe people are poor because of the choices they make that put them there. During my twenties, I graduated from college, found a job, got married, then had children. Those from this school would say that because I lived my life in the "right" way (embracing certain values), I didn't end up in poverty.

Others would say that it's great that some of us can live the "right" way, but many don't have that opportunity. Or, as the saying goes, "Life comes at you fast." They are proponents of the school-of-hard-knocks view of poverty. They argue that the biggest factor for a person living in poverty is the environment in which s/he lives.

I'm African American, and racism has not stopped me from achieving my economic goals. Yet that doesn't mean racism isn't hindering millions from achieving theirs. Every day, not only racism but classism, genderism, and other factors limit the opportunities and choices people have. And what if I do everything the "right" way and something beyond my control destroys my ability to generate income, leading me into poverty? The school-of-hard-knocks argument is that life choices are made within a context—and that context plays a big role in determining who lives in poverty. Maybe the most famous biblical account of riches to rags is that of Jesus' story of the prodigal son:

> There was a man who had two sons. The younger one said to his father, "Father, give me my share of the estate." So he divided his property between them.
>
> Not long after that, the younger son got together all he had, set off for a distant country and there squandered his wealth in wild living. After he had spent everything, there was a severe famine in that whole country, and he began to be in need. So he went and hired himself out to a citizen of that country, who sent him to his fields to feed pigs. He

longed to fill his stomach with the pods that the pigs were eating, but no one gave him anything. (Luke 15:11-16)

A variety of sins committed by the prodigal son landed him in poverty, the chief among them being arrogance. While it's true he had an inheritance coming (a third of his father's estate), it was disrespectful of him to ask for it while his father was still alive. It was like saying, "I wish you were dead." His request totally dismissed his father's position of authority as the head of the household.

Besides being arrogant, the prodigal son had no clue how to manage money. He went through it at a record pace. This led that trust fund baby to stoop to get the below-minimum-wage job of feeding pigs. Not only did the job not pay well, but it also cut him off from his heritage. Pigs also were considered unclean animals, which meant a righteous Jewish person wouldn't even touch them, let alone eat or use them in religious rituals. He ate the food that pigs ate, which also commonly served as the diet of the poor. He was stuck in poverty, and no other reason is given than his personal choices. So that's a point for the culture-of-poverty crowd.

For the school-of-hard-knocks crowd, there is a biblical principle of societal injustice—a concept that has shaped major themes in the Bible: The flood happened because societal sin was so out of control that God sent judgment (Genesis 6). Egypt was judged by God because they oppressed Israel (the book of Exodus). And if you believe the prophets, Israel was constantly in trouble—even sent into exile—because of their inability to be a just society. And what did Mary sing upon learning she would bear Jesus?

> He has brought down rulers from their thrones
>> but has lifted up the humble.
> He has filled the hungry with good things
>> but has sent the rich away empty. (Luke 1:52-53)

We could debate all day long, but it's pointless. The debate over the culture of poverty versus the school of hard knocks is of limited value for the church. I fear the debate is more about absolving responsibility to care for the poor in order to practice poverty shaming or greenlighting savior syndrome. Whether someone is there because s/he embraces a culture of poverty or is a graduate of the school of hard knocks, Scripture has a clear position: the church has a responsibility to play a role. Let's look at Deuteronomy 15:7-11.

> If anyone is poor among your fellow Israelites in any of the towns of the land the LORD your God is giving you, do not be hardhearted or tightfisted toward them. Rather, be open-handed and freely lend them whatever they need. Be careful not to harbor this wicked thought: "The seventh year, the year for canceling debts, is near," so that you do not show ill will toward the needy among your fellow Israelites and give them nothing. They may then appeal to the LORD against you, and you will be found guilty of sin. Give generously to them and do so without a grudging heart; then because of this the LORD your God will bless you in all your work and in everything you put your hand to. There will always be poor people in the land. Therefore I command you to be open-handed toward your fellow Israelites who are poor and needy in your land.

The principle expressed here is this: life has been hard for the poor, so honor them. God gave detailed instructions on how to help the poor in the Promised Land. In fact, it was part of the requirements for possessing it. Notice that there were no exceptions for those who were in poverty because of personal sin—no excuse at all to shut off the faucet of generosity. The command is clear: meet their needs, no matter what. The relentless stress in Scripture is on the condition of poverty being caused by sin on either personal and social levels. It's not either/or but both/and.

WHO ARE THE POOR?

The number-one reason people live in the condition of poverty in the United States is that they aren't employed in a job that pays well enough to keep them out of poverty. There are many reasons someone isn't gainfully employed, but lack of employment that provides enough personal income is the bottom line. In our country, there are clear indicators of who is likely to live in poverty. The more a person fits under the categories in the following list, the more likely he or she is living in poverty.[2]

+ *Service workers.* Ninety-five percent of people who live above the poverty line are employed full-time. However, it's not *if* you have a job but the type of job you have. Sixty-six percent of American workers who make minimum wage are in service occupations. If we assume a forty-hour workweek, minimum wage is not enough to bring someone with no dependents above the poverty line.

+ *Women.* It's no secret that women are paid less than men. One reason is because of the jobs they work. Another is because of genderism. For example, women with graduate degrees earn 71.9 percent of what men with similar education and experience earn. In addition, they're more likely than men to do things like provide unpaid caregiving services to the elderly and children.

+ *Latino/a.* People from this ethnic group experience an above-average rate of poverty. The two primary contributing factors are formal educational achievement and wage-earning levels. Only 16 percent have a bachelor's degree, and only 76.9 percent earn the median of all workers. In addition, 33 percent report employment discrimination.

+ *Kids under five.* In the United States, kids don't go to work, so their condition depends totally on what family they're born into. They are significantly more likely to be in poverty when compared to adults, and the youngest are the most vulnerable.

+ *Immigrants who aren't citizens.* About half of American immigrants have become citizens. Those who haven't are more likely to live in poverty, mainly due to the inability to find steady employment or to find anything but low-paying jobs. Immigrants who are undocumented have much higher poverty rates than other immigrants.

+ *African Americans.* This ethnic group is twice as likely to live in poverty than Asians or whites. Dating back to the institution of slavery, numerous intentional societal obstacles have made escaping poverty very difficult for them. While only making up one in eight Americans, they make up 25 percent of the poor population.

+ *Non-high-school graduates.* There is a big correlation between educational achievement and poverty level. That's because education is directly related to potential earnings. Those who didn't graduate from high school earn an average of $20,924 a year; those who did graduate from high school earn about $8,000 more; and those who graduated from college earn on average $51,094 annually.

+ *Native Americans.* The effects of four centuries of systemic oppression still resonate among this population. They have the highest poverty rate of any ethnic group, as a quarter of them live below the poverty line.

+ *The disabled.* Those who have a disability are more likely than most to not be able to work. Research shows that workplace discrimination plays a key role in keeping them from finding steady, livable-wage employment. Despite the enactment of American Disabilities Act (ADA), the unemployment gap between the disabled and those who are not continues to widen.

+ *New single mothers.* Anyone who has a child knows how much they cost. An incredible 44.3 percent of women in this category live in poverty. Most of these pregnancies were unplanned.

POVERTY IS NOT AN IDENTITY

The practice of poverty shaming needs to stop within the body of Christ.[3] We need to accept the fact that people are in poverty because they lack financial resources—it's no deeper than that. There are many complex reasons why they are in this condition—and it is a *condition.* Their circumstance may be long- or short-term, but "poor" is not their identity as a human being.

Seeing poverty as an *identity* makes the lives of the poor probationary. In society's eyes, they come off probation and become valuable only if they perform well against the challenge of living in poverty. Society's standard is this: if you can't overcome your deficits, you don't matter. Or worse, you matter *only* if you have a clear, defined deficit. Unfortunately, the standard for valuing people from the hood is based on deficits.

I recently received an advertisement in the mail for a local candidate for the school board. It's nicely done. It is a very appealing ad with a smiling African American man on the right side. On the left side is a door open to a classroom and the words "Gary Favors: Opening the Door to Opportunity." It then goes on to make an appeal as to why I should vote for him: "Growing up in Cincinnati's inner city, Gary beat the odds. He became the first in his family to go to college, served as a US Army Captain and has a 23-year record as a teacher in Cincinnati Public Schools. Gary has the vision and leadership our schools need." So the marketers did a great job of highlighting the standard overcoming-a-deficit narrative.

Now let me be clear. I am not against celebrating overcoming odds. If you go to the World Impact blog, you're going to see a ton of stories of people who have overcome. Gary's story is inspiring, and I'm glad he overcame. My whole ministry life has been about helping people overcome. What I'm questioning is why overcoming poverty is the standard narrative we use to value people in or from poverty.

Test me out on this. Go to any form of media and look up a story of someone from the hood. I guarantee that nine times out of ten it's a celebration of that person overcoming the deficits created by poverty: an athlete who grew up dirt poor and made it to the big leagues; an ex-con graduate from an Ivy League school; a single mother who started her own business. It's the standard society uses to determine the value of those from the hood.

For the church, this should not be our standard.

If the standards are the overcomers, and you are in poverty and you didn't overcome, the reasoning is *it must be your fault.* This attitude does not lead to compassion—and it is unbiblical. Reality is that most will not overcome. The Bible tells us the poor will always be with us (Matthew 26:11; Deuteronomy15:11). That is why we are to take a posture of *generosity* as our standard. A person's condition doesn't make her life any less valuable than the life of one who overcomes.

The prevailing attitude about the hood—an attitude that focuses on the deficits—is not good. Therefore, understanding the difference between poverty as *identity* and poverty as *condition* is the key to successful ministry in the hood.

Identity might be thought of as both the way we define ourselves internally and the way we represent ourselves to others. We all use social categories to communicate who we are. Some categories I frequently use are CEO, father, African American, and Christian. Each one of these categories symbolizes meaning, both privately and publicly. Others position me according to the categories I am identified with. And we indicate what's important to us by what category we put ourselves in. Both how we personally identify ourselves and how we are identified by society at large is no small matter.

For example, I live in Cincinnati. It's a major city with a town-like attitude. When people inquire about what school someone attended, they don't mean college; they mean high school. Once you give people that answer, you're immediately put in certain categories. You can tell which schools are held in high regard, because certain alumni state loud and proud where they went. On the other hand, when a person states the name of a school that's not highly thought of, s/he's likely to quickly explain why s/he went there—as if in apology. It's all about social positioning.

When we define ourselves, we publicly proclaim that we are like one group of people and not like others. This is necessary to communicate, yet it leads to two big challenges. First, using categories is nowhere near as clear-cut as we would like it to be. Social identities are always morphing and intertwined. A recent example is the meaning of *evangelical Christian*. To the general public, it used to mean conservative Christian. It has evolved to mean a white voting alliance. To address this, people say things like "Yes, I am evangelical, but I don't vote Republican." Or they refuse to embrace the term at all.

We may have more in common with people in categories we have defined ourselves by than with how society defines us. For example, a friend of mine coached AAU basketball, and he had a very talented white kid on the team. The kid told him many times essentially that he was black although he had white skin. Now, that didn't make him black. But he identified with black culture far more than with white culture.

The ways people in the hood are identified is a bigger problem than we realize. We all develop our identities because of our connections with certain social categories, but we also develop them in contrast to other categories. For example, what it means to be *rich* depends largely on what it means to be *poor*.

We need to understand that how we identify with those in poverty has a huge impact on how much we value them—and how we disciple them. If part of your identity as a church worker in the hood is to blame a person's poverty strictly on his own lack of effort, you will close yourself off to the numerous reasons the Bible provides for why people end up poor.

THE CONDITION OF POVERTY

The fact is, most people who are born into poverty don't switch social classes in their lifetime. If you never lived in it, but for the grace of God go you. No one should act like they hit a triple financially when they were born on third base. If you were born into a family that lives in a seedy apartment complex and grew up sharing a mattress in the middle of a living-room floor with your siblings, odds are you aren't going to grow up to go to Stanford and run a tech company.

I make that statement not as a commentary concerning the ability of the poor. Quite the contrary. It has everything to do with the odds stacked against them being able to live out their humanity as God intended. Kids in poverty experience a vicious cycle of moving, missing many school days, horrible housing, a constant threat of violence, undependable relationships, and a myriad of other challenges. I'm not listing these things as some ivory-tower academic (although with my credentials I can hang with the best of them). I'm writing from firsthand experience. I'm not guessing.

While pastoring in the hood for about a decade, I was the working poor. It was a financial condition I chose to be in so I could be a more effective minister. What I remember most about that time was the constant stress. So, frankly, it angers me when I hear speakers glorify the life of the poor. There was nothing glorious about it. Life was hard. Too many times I would have twenty-five dollars left to take care of my family until the next payday two weeks later. The joke in my house was that we fasted because we had no choice. There were many restless days and sleepless nights.

I don't believe anyone doubts that the hood is a troubled place. Tons of research outlines why. Most authors and experts point to the ebb and flow of various economic tides. Neighborhoods that were once vibrant because of plenteous tax revenue and employment opportunities based on industries were devastated when said industries went into decline. I can remember a friend of mine getting a living-wage job at Buckeye Steel straight out of high school. Nowadays he would more than likely have been employed in the service industry at a much lower wage.

So a narrative that focuses on the deficits of people who live in poverty is problematic. And the same could be said for the neighborhoods they live in. The road most traveled focuses on the problems of the community. When I say *poverty*, or maybe even *urban*, people's minds tend to drift to gangs, drugs, crime, etc. Politicians use the word as a dog whistle all the time. The lens used to view the community is almost always negative. It's as if nothing good can ever exist in the hood. Far too many times that is the accepted truth.

DEFICITS, DOLLARS, AND DEPENDENCE

Because of this, when it comes to seeking the common good of a neighborhood, there are a lot of dollars tied to viewing a community through a deficit lens. When I say common good, I mean activities that benefit the interests of all within the community. Because there is a lot of money tied to the deficits of the hood, they become atmospheres of aid in which the identity of the people is closely tied to being a dependent of some sort. Funding is rarely issued based on neighborhood residents solving their own problems. So they tend to look toward outsiders to become their heroes.

If you have ever filled out a grant request for the hood, you know this. If you want grant money, you must demonstrate just how bad things are. The more problems you can demonstrate, the more money available. Within the church world, I've sat at many urban-ministry fundraisers where the resilience of the residents was *never* celebrated. The whole program was focused on making the ministry worker the hero. The emphasis always seems to be on the goodwill provided instead of the talents of the people who live there.

As in other social classes, becoming a consumer dominates the person in poverty's activity—except it looks different. Survival is the focus, and it's a constant game of outwitting the system. Why? Because more times than not the system has locked them out. We need to offer opportunities to transcend this.

Transcendence requires that we view the condition of our lives in a more accurate way than what is common. In error, we look at circumstances; ponder what to do; and make God an adviser. When the condition becomes the identity, it determines the opportunity. As when we ask the question What would Jesus do? we may casually fall into the trap to make ourselves the moral standard by practicing the savior syndrome, as I discussed earlier. God should not shrink. In determining what should be done, we should not overrule God's teachings as it is not about us (see figure 2).

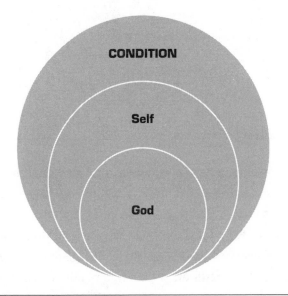

Figure 2. Making ourselves the standard

Let's go back to *In His Steps* and the question What would Jesus do? What most don't decipher is that Sheldon's characters were created with the assumption they are good theologians. In other words, the question is a guide toward transformation because they already know how to apply the teachings of Jesus properly—and *that's* the standard. Otherwise how can they determine if they walk in his steps? Looking at life this way puts circumstances in their proper place (see figure 3).

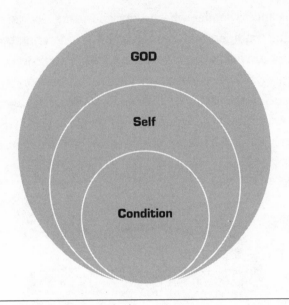

Figure 3. Making God the standard

The proper analysis of poverty—as with any condition we find ourselves in—is that God is primary; we are God's people, and God is bigger than *any* condition. The more we understand who God is, the better we understand who we are. Then we're more effective in responding in this broken world. That's empowerment.

People in the condition of poverty are not goodwill projects. They do not exist for us to fulfill our life purpose or any other desire we may have. Most people in poverty work, but there is more month than money. And their condition does not determine their destiny; they are made in the image of God like all of us. The church must offer an alternative to outwitting a corrupt system. We must offer our neighbors transcendence over their condition.

3

JESUS DID, NOT JESUS WOULD

JESUS AND THE CONDITION OF POVERTY

AN AMERICAN INVESTMENT BANKER was taking a much-needed vacation in a small coastal village on the coast of Mexico when a small boat with just one fisherman docked. The boat had several large, fresh fish in it. The investment banker was impressed by the quality of the fish and asked the fisherman how long it took to catch them. He replied, "Only a little while."

The banker then asked why he didn't stay out longer and catch more fish, and the fisherman replied he had enough to support his family's immediate needs. The American then asked, "But what do you do with the rest of your time?"

"I sleep late, fish a little, play with my children, take siesta with my wife, and I stroll into the village each evening, where I sip wine and play guitar with my amigos. I have a full and busy life, señor."

The investment banker scoffed. "I am an Ivy League MBA, and I could help you. You could spend more time fishing and with the proceeds buy a bigger boat. And with the proceeds from the bigger boat you could buy several boats until eventually you would have a whole fleet of fishing boats. Instead of selling your catch to the middleman, you could sell directly to the processor, eventually opening your own cannery. You could control the product, processing, and distribution."

He was silent for a moment then added, "Of course, you would need to leave this small coastal fishing village and move to Mexico City, where you would run your growing enterprise."

The fisherman asked, "But how long will this all take?"

"Fifteen or twenty years."

"But what then?"

The American laughed and said, "That's the best part. When the time is right, you would announce an IPO and sell your company stock to the public—and become very rich. You could make millions."

"Millions, señor? Then what?"

"Then you would retire. You could move to a small coastal fishing village where you would sleep late, fish a little, play with your kids, take siesta with your wife, stroll to the village in the evenings where you could sip wine and play your guitar with your amigos."[1]

I love this simple parable because it teaches that life should not revolve around what we gain materially. The fisherman was happy with the life he had, but the banker insisted that the only good life is a wealthy one. That is not at all biblical. The good life in Christ is meant for *all*.

Now, overall the Bible affirms the goodness of wealth (Genesis 1–2; Revelation 21–22). Jesus talked about money a lot, including encouraging us to make money (Luke 19:11-27; Matthew 25:14-30). And he never condemned the generosity of the people around him.

Yet it may come as a shock that overall Jesus didn't have many good things to say about the wealthy. That's not my opinion but the honest assessment of many theologians who have forgotten more than I will ever know about the subject of wealth. This chapter is a brief observation of some key takeaways about Jesus and wealth.

JESUS WAS THE WORKING POOR

The fact that Jesus was from the hood is significant. The fact that he lived his life in the condition of poverty makes an emphatic point about God's attitude toward social status.

Christianity is a poor person's religion; most people who claim the faith globally are impoverished. According to the Center for the Study of Global Christianity, 81 percent of Christians live on less than one hundred dollars a day. The present face of Christianity is a nonwhite woman living in the global South, with lower-than-average levels of societal safety and proper health care.[2] This fact is typically lost on us in the United States. The way Jesus chose to live is a demonstration of the reality that in God's kingdom there is no hierarchy based on social class. Instead the way toward status in the kingdom is faith, service, and obedience.

Jesus grew up in Nazareth, which was like the hood. When Nathanael heard that Jesus was from there, he was shocked. He wondered out loud if anything good could come out of such a place (John 1:46). It was a small, obscure, and detached town on the outskirts of the massive city of Sepphoris, which people were proud to be from. Nobody Jewish bragged about being from Nazareth. To them, it was the home of the occupying Roman army base.

Jesus was an everyday man. We must get those pretty Christmas card scenes of Jesus being born in spectacular fashion in a bright, cheery stable out of our heads. Instead think of a dark, smelly basement room used to house animals. *Manger* is a fancy word for dinner plate for the animals. Not one of us would want our children born in those conditions. This isn't how the wealthy enter the world. Jesus entered in the humblest, most ordinary way imaginable.

There were several ceremonies that a Jewish family went through after the birth of a baby (Luke 2:21-24). If it was a male, the baby was circumcised after eight days and dedicated to God after one month. After forty days, the parents were to bring a lamb, dove, or pigeon for a sin offering. The fact that Mary and Joseph offered a pair of doves or two young pigeons indicates their financial condition; only rich people brought lambs. Jesus clearly did not grow up in a condition of abundance. In fact, it seems he lived his whole life in poverty.

Also consider this:

> When Jesus saw the crowd around him, he gave orders to cross to the other side of the lake. Then a teacher of the law came to him and said, "Teacher, I will follow you wherever you go." Jesus replied, "Foxes have dens and birds have nests, but the Son of Man has no place to lay his head." Another disciple said to him, "Lord, first let me go and bury my father." But Jesus told him, "Follow me, and let the dead bury their own dead." (Matthew 8:18-22)

This passage gives remarkable insight into Jesus' mindset concerning the pursuit of wealth rather than eternal things. At this point, Jesus was an up-and-coming rabbi or "teacher of the law." Rabbis were experts in how to handle documentation and interpret laws, of which the Jews had many. They were a big deal because they were literate among illiterate people. They were expected to be experts in the Scriptures.

This person asked Jesus to disciple him, to be his rabbi. And Jesus warned him that he was a different type of rabbi. Traditional rabbis had a high standard of living. They usually had a prestigious school or synagogue and held a place of honor within society. Jesus' answer that "foxes have dens and birds have nests, but the Son of Man has no place to lay his head" implied that the man shouldn't expect worldly status to come from following him. Jesus had no school or synagogue, and he had no plans of starting one. He didn't even have a house! But he was not homeless. He depended on the generosity of friends, relatives, associates, and neighbors who believed in his mission. This is evidence that throughout his ministry, Jesus continued the life of working poverty he had grown up in.

Here's a natural question that comes up: as church workers, what should our posture be concerning living with the poor? Some believe that to really be like Jesus, we must be incarnational like he was and live as impoverished people. I believe Jesus answered this question in the following.

> Just then a man came up to Jesus and asked, "Teacher, what good thing must I do to get eternal life?"
>
> "Why do you ask me about what is good?" Jesus replied. "There is only One who is good. If you want to enter life, keep the commandments."
>
> "Which ones?" he inquired.
>
> Jesus replied, "'You shall not murder, you shall not commit adultery, you shall not steal, you shall not give false testimony, honor your father and mother,' and 'love your neighbor as yourself.'"

"All these I have kept," the young man said. "What do I still lack?"

Jesus answered, "If you want to be perfect, go, sell your possessions and give to the poor, and you will have treasure in heaven. Then come, follow me."

When the young man heard this, he went away sad, because he had great wealth. (Matthew 19:16-22)

There are two legitimate ways we could interpret why the rich young ruler went away sad. The first is that he loved his possessions so much he knew he couldn't part with them. Therefore, he couldn't follow Jesus. That's the most common interpretation. However, you can also interpret that he loved Jesus so much, he was committed to selling everything he had. He went away sad because he realized how hard his life was about to become. This isn't the common interpretation in American culture, but it isn't wrong either.

Scripture is silent on what the young man did with the advice he received. Regardless of what he did, the principle is the same: don't let wealth obstruct your ability to follow Jesus. I don't think we have to sell everything to follow God. That includes doing effective ministry among the poor. In the circles I run in, this view is dubious. But I don't think there should be a war between the two positions. We should all be *willing* to live in poverty like Jesus did, if that's what it takes. There was a season in my life when that's exactly what I did.

If you think God is calling you to live among the poor, go do it. But do it a certain way; make a choice. Consult resources about how to live incarnationally among the poor in a healthy way. If you don't do this properly, you'll be a colonizer. I've seen many people move into the hood under the guise of ministry, but they are just participants in the present wave of gentrification. If your thought is *I hope I never have to live among the poor*, review your life and consider whether you're too attached to your possessions and social status. That's a situation of the heart that only you and God can address.

JESUS FAVORED THE POOR

When it comes to Christ's second coming, Scripture emphasizes three things: First, when he comes back, it will be unexpected. Second, we are to be prepared. And third, we will be held accountable for how we lived. Jesus made it clear there will be a separation of true believers and fake followers (see Matthew 25:31-46). The evidence he will use is how we behaved. If we say we love God, it will be reflected in our love for people. Our actions will be the scoreboard of what we *really* believe.

In Matthew 25, Jesus gave assurances and warnings about what will happen upon his second coming. The stress was on the behaviors of people who will not inherit his kingdom. He started by putting people in two categories: sheep and goats. The sheep are the people of God; the goats are those who are not.

In Matthew 25:35, we see why the sheep are blessed: they took care of him when he was hungry, thirsty, a stranger, naked, sick, and in prison. Interestingly the sheep are confused. They want to know when they did those things? Jesus answered that when they served the people who were the neediest among them, they served him. The sheep displayed the love of God regardless of who needed it. Jesus' sheep are certainly supposed to care for one another, but they are *especially* supposed to take responsibility for those in poverty.

Jesus then turned his attention toward the goats. He flat-out condemned them for their actions. They will be punished for not caring for him physically. And like the sheep, the goats are confused. When did they commit such a hateful act? When they ignored the neediest among them, they did not do the right thing. Their hearts were not right, and their not being generous was the evidence that convicted them.

Remember, this parable is tied to our coming judgment, so we shouldn't take this lesson lightly. One of the ways Jesus will hold us accountable when we die and see him is by our actions toward those in need. If we're truly committed to Christ, some part of the evidence is how we treat the poor in our lifetime. I would go so far as to say that if you aren't committing some amount of time, talent, and/or treasure toward those in poverty, do not let another day go by without doing so. That is how serious this teaching is.

THE POVERTY OF JOHN THE BAPTIST

John the Baptist played the specific role of preparing the way for Jesus' ministry. He was a great teacher in his own right, constantly preaching repentance. He tied proof of repentance to a person's level of generosity, and he stressed contentment with what one owns (Luke 3:11-14). When John was in doubt about whether his cousin Jesus was truly the Messiah, Jesus included proclaiming the good news to the poor as evidence that he was the real deal (Luke 7:22). In the gospel of Luke, we also find the story of Jesus being rejected in his hometown hood of Nazareth (Isaiah 61:1-3, proclaimed by Jesus in Luke 4:16-28).

> The Spirit of the Sovereign LORD is on me,
>> because the LORD has anointed me
>> to proclaim good news to the poor.
> He has sent me to bind up the brokenhearted,
>> to proclaim freedom for the captives
>> and release from darkness for the prisoners,

> to proclaim the year of the Lord's favor
>
>> and the day of vengeance of our God,
>
> to comfort all who mourn,
>
>> and provide for those who grieve in Zion.

What got him in trouble was when he declared, "Today this Scripture is fulfilled." He was claiming to be the son of God, and that comment went over like a lead balloon. Ironically, like Nathanael, the very citizens of Nazareth began to question if something good could come from there, especially the Messiah. His sermon angered them so much they wanted to throw him off a cliff. Too often, commentary on the word *poor* in this sermon is super-spiritualized to mean something other than people who don't have money.

We must not lose sight of the fact Jesus followed up this sermon by demonstrating what he meant by the words he spoke. His actions showed he clearly meant embracing the financially poor. If we closely follow the stories presented in the accounts of Matthew, Mark, Luke, and John, we see that it's often the rich who opposed him. The least, the last, and the lost of the backwater hoods he preached in (not unlike where he grew up) were his audience. He went to everyday people everywhere.

The Sermon on the Mount provides clear teaching on the expectations Jesus has for his followers (Matthew 5–7). This is the longest continuous teaching of Jesus we have on record. He made several points within the sermon, but let's focus on his thoughts on giving to those in need and what our attitudes should be about money. For example, he said,

> Be careful not to practice your righteousness in front of others to be seen by them. If you do, you will have no reward from your Father in heaven.

So when you give to the needy, do not announce it with trumpets, as the hypocrites do in the synagogues and on the streets, to be honored by others. Truly I tell you, they have received their reward in full. But when you give to the needy, do not let your left hand know what your right hand is doing, so that your giving may be in secret. Then your Father, who sees what is done in secret, will reward you. (Matthew 6:1-4)

Let's start by recognizing the matter-of-fact nature of his statement. It's not a choice of *if* you should give to the needy but *when*. Like John the Baptist, Jesus tied our faith to our ability to be generous. And that generosity should come from pure motives, not selfish ones. When we give the right way, we aren't hypocritical. Our motives should come from a sincere heart.

Let's be honest; it's easier to do the right thing when we know we will be praised for doing it. That's why we're encouraged to give to the poor without fanfare and to do so not expecting anything in return. If we follow those guidelines and our hearts are at peace, that's an indication that our motives are in the right place.

JESUS WARNED AGAINST RICHES

In his Sermon on the Mount, Jesus also gave us a warning against materialism:

Do not store up for yourselves treasures on earth, where moths and vermin destroy, and where thieves break in and steal. But store up for yourselves treasures in heaven, where moths and vermin do not destroy, and where thieves do not break in and steal. For where your treasure is, there your heart will be also.

The eye is the lamp of the body. If your eyes are healthy, your whole body will be full of light. But if your eyes are

unhealthy, your whole body will be full of darkness. If then
the light within you is darkness, how great is that darkness!

No one can serve two masters. Either you will hate the one
and love the other, or you will be devoted to the one and
despise the other. You can't serve both God and money.
(Matthew 6:19-24)

There is only one thing that can master us on the level that
Jesus can: money. A life chasing after money is a dead one. I have
the privilege of meeting a lot of people and gaining many life-
enriching experiences. I rarely meet people who don't tie their
homes, neighborhoods, cars, and other materialistic blessings
into their identity. But every now and then I meet someone who
is free from this, choosing to live beneath his or her level of income.

Sadly, it never dawns on most of us that there's a biblical principle of limiting riches and poverty. Some think I'm making a political statement against the wealthy. If you're in that camp, I ask
that you suspend your assumptions and be open to the truth that
many Scriptures teach: there is such a thing as being in an un-
ethical state of having too much materially. Where that line is,
Scripture is not clear. But we need to recognize that a threshold
exists and to guard our hearts against it constantly.

Someone in the crowd said to Jesus, "Teacher, tell my brother
to divide the inheritance with me." Jesus replied, "Man, who
appointed me a judge or an arbiter between you?" Then he
said to them, "Watch out! Be on your guard against all kinds
of greed; life does not consist in an abundance of possessions."

And he told them this parable: "The ground of a certain
rich man yielded an abundant harvest. He thought to himself,
'What shall I do? I have no place to store my crops.' Then he
said, 'This is what I'll do. I will tear down my barns and build
bigger ones, and there I will store my surplus grain. And I'll

say to myself, "You have plenty of grain laid up for many years. Take life easy; eat, drink and be merry."

"But God said to him, 'You fool! This very night your life will be demanded from you. Then who will get what you have prepared for yourself?' This is how it will be with whoever stores up things for themselves but is not rich toward God." (Luke 12:13-21)

In this passage, Jesus addressed the attitude we should have about money: our life purpose lies outside wealth. His message is "Don't put your identity in that condition. Instead put it in your relationship with me."

That is the heart of the matter for both rich and poor, and it goes against our natural inclinations. Jesus said money has no owners, just spenders. The good life in Christ is available to all, not just those outside poverty. Don't desire what you don't have, as that leads to the sin of greed.

It's only human to root our identity in our financial position, to rest our security in the fact that money gives a certain measure of control over the quality of our lives. But if you think the amount of money you've accumulated directly correlates to the purpose and meaning of your life, you don't own your bank account; your bank account owns you.

The rich man's death in this story is tragic because it seems he had no plans for his surplus other than to enrich himself further. Yet this isn't a parable against accumulating money. In other places in Scripture, we are told it is wise to practice financial planning. The warning is about the seduction of wealth. We came into this world with nothing, and we will leave the same way. Therefore, while we're here, we are to be sure to use money to help others. We do so by investing in things that are eternal. Jesus modeled and spoke of this attitude.

> Then Jesus said to his host, "When you give a luncheon or dinner, do not invite your friends, your brothers or sisters, your relatives, or your rich neighbors; if you do, they may invite you back and so you will be repaid. But when you give a banquet, invite the poor, the crippled, the lame, the blind, and you will be blessed. Although they can't repay you, you will be repaid at the resurrection of the righteous." (Luke 14:12-14)

We can't be good Christians unless we are humble. Nothing brings about humility like the steady practice of generosity. We are never to practice a *quid pro quo*, giving in order to receive. Want to be countercultural? Don't cater to gain favor from those who can make you more financially comfortable. Of course, they need Jesus too, but be careful not to seek them out for your own benefit. Rather engage them in kingdom purposes.

If we don't seek honor, in due time God will honor us. True generosity is not an even exchange. Yet when we intentionally seek to serve people who have no way to repay us, our kindness will likely be repaid. So if you want to follow Jesus, go *beyond*. Be hospitable to the outcasts of society. Want to be blessed? Bless the neediest among you with no expectation of repayment. God sees you, and that should be enough.

JESUS CONDEMNED THE ABUSE OF WEALTH

Jesus taught that spiritual and material matters are inseparable. Eternal consequences arise from decisions we make about material goods and what place they have in our lives. Jesus didn't just suggest that we practice generosity. If we believe his teachings, our faith depends on it. Earlier we looked at Matthew 19:16-22. Let's now look at the rest of the story.

> Then Jesus said to his disciples, "Truly I tell you, it is hard for someone who is rich to enter the kingdom of heaven. Again

I tell you, it is easier for a camel to go through the eye of a needle than for someone who is rich to enter the kingdom of God."

When the disciples heard this, they were greatly astonished and asked, "Who then can be saved?"

Jesus looked at them and said, "With man this is impossible, but with God all things are possible."

Peter answered him, "We have left everything to follow you! What then will there be for us?"

Jesus said to them, "Truly I tell you, at the renewal of all things, when the Son of Man sits on his glorious throne, you who have followed me will also sit on twelve thrones, judging the twelve tribes of Israel. And everyone who has left houses or brothers or sisters or father or mother or wife or children or fields for my sake will receive a hundred times as much and will inherit eternal life. But many who are first will be last, and many who are last will be first." (Matthew 19:23-30)

Jesus appeared to be teaching that it's impossible for the rich to enter the kingdom, and this startled his followers. The common belief was that the rich were saved because of their bank account; their riches were a sure sign of God's blessing. He assured them that, yes, the rich can enter in, but their riches were not the access code. Just like everyone else, their salvation came by faith and how they live it out. We will be rewarded for our faith and service, regardless of wealth. Jesus told this story to illustrate that fact.

"There was a rich man who was dressed in purple and fine linen and lived in luxury every day. At his gate was laid a beggar named Lazarus, covered with sores and longing to eat what fell from the rich man's table. Even the dogs came and licked his sores.

"The time came when the beggar died and the angels carried him to Abraham's side. The rich man also died and was buried. In Hades, where he was in torment, he looked up and saw Abraham far away, with Lazarus by his side. So he called to him, 'Father Abraham, have pity on me and send Lazarus to dip the tip of his finger in water and cool my tongue, because I am in agony in this fire.'

"But Abraham replied, 'Son, remember that in your lifetime you received your good things, while Lazarus received bad things, but now he is comforted here and you are in agony. And besides all this, between us and you a great chasm has been set in place, so that those who want to go from here to you can't, nor can anyone cross over from there to us.'

"He answered, 'Then I beg you, father, send Lazarus to my family, for I have five brothers. Let him warn them, so that they will not also come to this place of torment.'

"Abraham replied, 'They have Moses and the Prophets; let them listen to them.'" (Luke 16:19-29)

The sickly beggar Lazarus, who we would think is not blessed by God, receives a reward, while the rich man, who was considered blessed, is penalized. We can't conclude that the rich man went to hell because of his wealth alone. Yet we can deduce that refusing to care for Lazarus when he clearly had the means to do so was not right. For Jesus, both the amount of money we have *and* how we use it are important. He flipped the script on us. He's clear that the last shall be first and the first shall be last.

For three decades, I have had breakfast with Bob a few times a year.[3] When we get together, we do what I call the three Fs—discuss our faith, reminisce about our friendship, and discuss my ministry future.

We met by happenstance. It was my first day on the job in 1995, fresh out of Bible college at a place called City CURE. Bob was in my colleague's office and shared with me his vision to sponsor a church plant in the inner city of Cincinnati one day. *What a great idea,* I thought as I left our initial encounter. Little did I know that five years later I would be that church planter.

Bob was a businessman who felt that the reason God blessed him with wealth was to give most of it away. He has given over $100,000 to my former church plant, and that's just one of the ways he gives. His life is the greatest example of financial generosity I have ever seen.

As a minister of the gospel, one thing has become clear to me. When God wants something done in the hood, he raises up people like Bob. Many Christians in his financial position have a longing to do something beyond build wealth. They see being generous as a ministry calling. They live out a theology of enough.

What did Jesus do? It may be hard to accept, but he played favorites. He lived his whole life among the poor. This enabled him to feel their pain. He also made clear that they are to be preferred in ministry. He warned that we not let the chase for riches seduce us. If we aren't careful, that chase will consume use. We will be held accountable for how we treat the poor. Jesus also condemned the abuse of wealth. How will you apply these principles to your life?

4

THE PEOPLE OF GOD

GOD'S PLAN FOR A BROKEN WORLD

I'M THE THIRD PRESIDENT OF WORLD IMPACT. Our founding president was a highly influential person. The second president served as a bridge between World Impact's past and its present. Everyone—from members of the board of directors to volunteers—has an opinion or story about our founder. His shadow looms over our ministry, for better or worse. The better part is that God used him to start a powerful ministry.

If you are a DC or Marvel fan, you're familiar with the concept of an origin story: the circumstances in which a superhero gains his superpowers. In Los Angeles, God inspired a white teenager to start Bible clubs for poor African American kids. He recruited hundreds of others to join him. They earned the respect of the community—so much so that when the Watts Riots happened while the kids clubs was meeting, *none* of the white leaders of the kids club were harmed. During that riot, thirty-four people died and more than three thousand were arrested. Almost fifty years later, that movement that started as Bible clubs still exists, empowering grassroots urban leaders across the globe.

Now the worst. Later that white leader committed a moral failure, and his exit was not graceful. Many were hurt and felt betrayed. Although this transpired some time ago, our ministry is still in recovery mode in some ways. Indeed, his legacy is a mixed bag.

Within this backdrop I sought the Lord concerning the relationship World Impact should have with its founder. I received wise counsel from both inside and outside our ministry. Most importantly, I prayed, studied the Scriptures, and drew the conclusion that World Impact should not be divided. So I sought reconciliation. Why am I telling you this story? Because I want to demonstrate the importance of holiness. We owe every person we lead and serve our best efforts toward pursuing it.

Successful leadership involves pursuing personal holiness, strategic planning, talent development, and resource acquisition. Of these four, personal holiness far outweighs the others. When moral failures happen, it's like dropping a boulder into a body of water. The ripples shatter the peaceful waters, and the lack of peace flows out in an ever-widening circle. What happened to World Impact has killed many other ministries. That's because too many haven't valued personal holiness, so too many boulders have dropped.

Crossing the line from leading and doing ministry to *owning* a ministry is one of the clearest pathways to moral failure. When we own a ministry, we aren't capable of giving the neighborhood or the people we lead and serve everything needed to be successful. They don't belong to us; they belong to God. We must always believe that the foundation of the church is holiness—and act on that belief.

CANCEL CULTURE

In this age of cancel culture, individuals, institutions, and groups are publicly shamed for demonstrating or even just affirming an unpopular opinion or cultural value. When mass disapproval of the behavior occurs, they are "cancelled." If you participate in social media, you've seen this in action. At the very least, this leads to bad short-term publicity for the "offender"; long-term, it means a loss of influence. However, most of the time there's just aimless outrage that's over soon. Few of the people or groups that have been targeted experience long-term consequences.

The body of Christ is not immune to this, including those of us who work with the poor. I find too many are canceling the church. Some are quite vocal with their criticism and critique, and there is a place for that. But there also is a danger zone where criticism reaches such a fever pitch that it becomes crushing accusation. We need to be mindful of this, because Satan doesn't need any help (Revelation 12:10). When I hear accusations, I always wonder what God thinks.

God can't be pleased with this tendency toward accusation in our Christian culture. After all, he calls the church his bride (Ephesians 5:25-27). If you talk about *my* bride negatively, the first time I may be cordial and let it slide. The second time, I'll let you know it's not cool. The third time, those are fighting words. Crossing the line from critique to accusation leads to undervaluing the church and turning to things like politics playing a role it's not built to play. This seems to be birthed out of disillusionment and/or an unclear view of the purpose of the church. Politics has its role, as it is *a* way to practice advocacy, but only the church is *the* way.

Someone comes in to try to save the hood. A devastating experience (or experiences) happens that leads that person to heartbreak. When the cape comes off, and the person figures out it can't save the hood, they arrive at a spiritual crossroads. That's where a war over what they know about the hood, the sovereignty of God, and the authority of the Bible takes place. Theirs is a collision between idealism and reality. And instead of choosing to work through the pain associated with ministry, they begin a slow slide into universalism or humanism.

You can't do sustainable ministry unless you have a practical theology of the poor. The church is all you have, and it's all you need. Most would agree the normal church experience is nurturing, fulfilling, and nontoxic, even if imperfect. Not every church harms its flock. That's why it's a travesty to reject the church as an answer for the hood. Most who take the road toward humanism or universalism came in with a savior syndrome and were not grounded in what the death, burial, and resurrection of Jesus Christ really means.

It's almost as if Jesus were a mascot for advocacy. My main pound-the-table point when I talk with people doing work in the hood is that the neighborhood doesn't need more of you; it needs the faith you have in Christ. If the faith is not there, you will not last—nor will the ministry.

We won't be able to fix all the brokenness we find. And we can't save the hood by just pursuing the common good. There aren't enough good intentions in us to overcome those we encounter. The only route to our survival is to live in the tension of embracing the limits of our human ability and trusting in God to handle the flat-out impossible situations that are constantly presented.

One of my favorite professors in seminary would always discuss the most important part of our ministry. It wasn't strategy or skill sets, although those are important. It was the lost art of being with God. Our effectiveness in the hood requires that we be change agents. Change agents don't like to *be* anything; we *do*. When you get a group of us in the room, debates are had, plans get written, and things get done. It's all great, but we must be careful to *do* based on *being* with God.

A key verse for understanding this concept is 1 Peter 1:16: "Be holy, because I am holy." Yet being holy isn't something we can *do*. It's something we must *be*. It's the one thing that must happen every single day. When we think about how to make the world a better place, if we rely only on human ingenuity, we're leaving our greatest weapon out of the mix—that is, the Holy Spirit.

WELCOME, HOLY SPIRIT

We describe God the Father as love and Jesus as the prince of peace. Love and peace make us feel good about things. But when we refer to the Holy Spirit, we use words like *wind, fire, water*—impersonal words. Yet the best way to describe the Holy Spirit is as a person. It's important that we see the Holy Spirit as a person because a person has *presence*.

Have you ever been in a situation when somebody didn't acknowledge your presence? One time my wife and I went into a car dealership to look into buying a car. It was a weekday, and the dealership wasn't particularly busy. There were more salespeople than customers. We started to look at some cars in the showroom, and after about five minutes, we still hadn't been waited on. I saw one group of salespeople talking among themselves and another hanging at their desks. I thought, *Okay, eventually one of them is going to notice us and approach.*

Another five minutes passed. We were the only customers in the showroom, and an army of folk was ignoring us. Smoke is coming out of my ears, and I march up to one of the groups and demand to see the manager. Of course, everybody is apologetic and starts to serve us.

Why did I get mad? Because nobody wants to be made to feel invisible. We exist, and we want to be acknowledged. That's the courtesy you pay people because they are *real.*

Understanding the Spirit as a person means you think he is real. Christ put a human face on the Spirit, as they are interdependent. The coming of the Holy Spirit changes everything because he is the personal presence of God. And the presence of God is what changes things.

That presence is labeled *holiness.* Holiness displays the character of God and sets one apart for service of God. When we are made holy, we gain the privilege of influencing situations for God's glory. One example of a holy person is John the Baptist, who was set apart for God's service. He was called a righteous and holy man (Mark 6:20). Notice that the description is of what he *is,* not of what he is doing. His lifestyle showed both that he was set apart and that he reflected who God is.

When we focus on being holy, doing ministry in the hood means guarding our hearts from sin by practicing self-care. We make sure that fellow believers hold us accountable for our actions. We know we can't do it on your own and must actively collaborate with others. We know our job is to disciple people in the hood to bring out the best in them. We engage injustice for the sake of Christ. And we know that our small actions will lead to big impact. Being holy is being the church.

GOD'S PLAN

When the word *church* is used, most think of a building.[1] When I talk about church planting in the hood, my listeners often respond with something like, "There's a church building on every corner. We already have too many." But I have yet to have anyone point out to me where in Scripture there is a limit on how many churches we are to have in the world. And I always reply, "I'm not talking about *buildings.*"

In Genesis 2, we see God's plan for unity in the Garden of Eden. Relationships were perfect between people and God, among people themselves, and with the environment. The word *blessed* does not accurately describe what was going on. A better word is a Hebrew one, *shalom. Shalom* means all living things being in a state of completeness in every aspect of existence.

Take a moment to do this little exercise: Write down every need you and the hood have. After compiling your list, imagine if every need disappeared forever. That's *shalom.* In the garden of Eden, Adam and Eve experienced it.

But then the familiar story in Genesis 3 reaches the point when the whole situation unraveled, beginning the dysfunctional mess of an earth we have today. By *mess* I mean the lack of shalom, the dysfunction that occurred in the character of humans, which was brought about by the willful disobedience of Adam and Eve. With their sin, God's original intent for us—to live in unity—was violated.

Because of the fall, confidence was replaced by doubt. Honesty was replaced by deception. Intimacy was replaced by shame. Fellowship was replaced by fear. Barriers went up between Adam and Eve and between both of them and God. Along with the barriers came hostility. God questioned Adam, Adam blamed Eve, and Eve blamed the snake. In doing so, Adam and Eve showed the first signs of human conflict and rebellion against God, a rebellion that continues to have far-reaching effects.

Then God spoke to the evil being (represented by the serpent) that had started it all:

> And I will put enmity
>> between you and the woman,

> and between your offspring and hers;
>
> he will crush your head,
>
> and you will strike his heel. (Genesis 3:15)

This is the first hint of the church, foretelling a continual conflict between humans and representatives of evil. The battle lines were formed, and until Christ's return, the world will struggle in conflict. The apostle Paul called this time between the fall and Christ's return "the present evil age" (Galatians 1:4). Traditionally Genesis 3:15 is also interpreted as a foreshadowing of Christ's eventual defeat of Satan. We know that Christ came to reconcile people to their God, to each other, and to creation.

Let's now reflect on how Christ entered the world. A good place to start is Abraham and Sarah. God said,

> I will make you into a great nation
>
> and I will bless you;
>
> I will make your name great,
>
> and you will be a blessing.
>
> I will bless those who bless you,
>
> and whoever curses you I will curse
>
> and all peoples on earth
>
> will be blessed through you. (Genesis 12:2-3)

We see once again God's desire for unity: a unified nation bringing blessing to all.

Yet to receive the promise of God, Abraham had to make a few choices. All those choices boiled down to whether he was going to trust God and obey the call on his life. He had to act in faith. God brought even more clarity to his plan for using Abraham and Sarah to restore unity as he declared they would have a son, and he would fulfill the promise of blessing for all the people of the world (see Genesis 15).

God reminded Abraham's son Isaac of that promise and then reminded Isaac's son Jacob of the promise as well (Genesis 26:4; 28:4). The very existence of a genealogy is a confirmation of the promise. But the tangible blessing doesn't come overnight. After Genesis, the story expands beyond individuals to the complete sum of Abraham's offspring, which eventually becomes known as the nation of Israel. In Exodus we see the pitting of nation against nation as a contest between gods.

For example, the famous biblical plagues were each a contest between the God of Israel and one of Egypt's gods (Exodus 1–12). When God rescued the Israelites, he delivered the message that the God of Israel is the sovereign God over all, regardless of a person's ethnicity. As more and more non-Israelites recognized this, they switched allegiances. Consider Joshua 2 and the story of Rahab; read the story of Naomi and Ruth in the book of Ruth; ponder God's message to the Israelite captives in Babylon (Jeremiah 29:4-7). Throughout the Old Testament, the message to the Israelites was clear: they were God's people.

We see from this brief look at the Old Testament that the main avenue God uses to reveal himself is the witness of his people: Abraham's biological descendants, the nation of Israel. Part of the responsibility of the Israelites was to display God's character. Non-Israelites would see their behavior as a reflection of the true God of the universe. In the New Testament, the witness is expanded. The apostle Paul made it clear when he reminded the Galatians that they began their relationship with God the same way Abraham did: by faith (Galatians 3:6-9). Abraham's real offspring are those who have faith in his God, not those who inherit his blood.

The redemption of Christ permits *all* to enjoy the blessing of Abraham (v. 14). No longer do people need to seek out Israelites and convert to Judaism. That was the old paradigm. We are now told to receive the promise of the Spirit and to form communities of Spirit-filled people—the church. These communities are the primary vehicles for people to know God.

The focus of the New Testament is a community of people making its presence known by living differently. You can find examples of this in all the books Paul authored. His instructions on living the Christian life aren't geared toward individuals but toward the community of believers called the church. This is no small concern, as nothing less than the essence of the gospel is at stake.

Jesus set a clear pattern concerning how the gospel was going to spread—that is, by people influencing others to follow him through the witness of their lives as a gathered local community. First there were twelve (John 1:35-50); then seventy-two (Luke 10:1); then at least 120 (Acts 1:15); then more than three thousand (Acts 2:41); then millions—all through the simple concept of believers forming local groups and living differently from the world around them. We are citizens of the kingdom of God, a holy nation that acts as ambassadors of reconciliation to a conflicted world in rebellion (2 Corinthians 5:11-21).

I WILL BUILD MY CHURCH

People aren't saved just to go to heaven. God is creating a people. We can't lose sight of this. Unfortunately too many have reduced the salvation story to a simple formula of "God made the world, we are sinners, so God sent Jesus to save each of us from our sins." Creation, sin, Jesus, and that's a wrap!

Some wonder, *Well, what's wrong with that?* Here's what's wrong: the creation-sin-Jesus formula leads to a hyper-individualized

Christianity, with our faith being exclusively about our personal lives. Jesus becomes an ecclesiastical bellhop to serve me, myself, and I. We cheapen the gospel message to crass consumption.

The Bible provides an in-depth story, not a simple formula. When we confess Jesus Christ, we are confessing the world-changing idea that Christ came to die for sins, defeat Satan and destroy his works, and reestablish the reign of God in the earth. That's the work Jesus did with his life, death, burial, and resurrection. From the book of Acts on, the New Testament is written under the assumption that you are living in community with others within the confines of a local church. Salvation is personal but it's to be lived out communally.

What makes the church different from all other societal institutions? The holiness factor. Holiness is the way to victory. It's the empowering ingredient that destroys sin and makes room for transformation. It's what makes us God's people. Our faith in Christ provides access to this. The same power that raised Jesus from the dead is the source for renovating lives and communities.

The first twelve chapters of Acts tells the story of the formation of the church. The first key figure is Peter. This should come as no surprise, as when Peter confessed his belief that Jesus was God's son, Jesus told him that he would be a key church planter (Matthew 16:18).

After the resurrection, Christ invested forty days into his followers. During this time, the power source of the Holy Spirit was revealed. Jesus taught about the kingdom of God and that all believers are to live as citizens of it. What made it possible was the presence of the Holy Spirit. He taught them that the kingdom would not come until he returned a second time to defeat evil once and for all. Until then, all his followers are to work to expand God's kingdom, and the vehicle to do that is the local church.

WE'RE ON A MISSION

The Spirit not only gave birth to the church, it also is the source of its effectiveness. The apostle Paul wrote, "For we were all baptized by one Spirit so as to form one body—whether Jews or Gentiles, slave or free—and we were all given the one Spirit to drink. Even so the body is not made up of one part but of many" (1 Corinthians 12:13). The church is the answer for people from all walks of life. In the kingdom, race, social class, gender, talents, and abilities do not create hierarchies. The church is the place where things happen, and there is a place for you in it. In Corinth, differences divided the congregation. Paul admonished them not to let this be the case. Previously he wrote, "We were all given the one Spirit to drink," which means the church is a family.

In fact, the church is to be a fellowship of the Spirit. The disciples were to rally around the one thing they had in common, which was faith in Christ. That would usher in the presence of the Holy Spirit. Galatians 5:22-23 tells us what the presence of the Spirit brings: "But the fruit of the Spirit is love, joy, peace, forbearance, kindness, goodness, faithfulness, gentleness and self-control. Against such things there is no law." This environment occurs naturally in the Sprit's presence. When Christ's Spirit is activated, we can expect these things to be in abundance.

The Holy Spirit creates the proper environment for community and also is the source of the church's power. This was made clear in Acts 1:8: "But you will receive power when the Holy Spirit comes on you; and you will be my witnesses in Jerusalem, and in all Judea and Samaria, and to the ends of the earth." The difference in the lives of the disciples before the Spirit and after the Spirit is stark. Upon Christ's death, they moved in the shadows, not sure what to make of things. After spending time with Christ and being empowered by the Spirit, they risked their lives to spread the gospel and establish churches throughout the Roman Empire and beyond. They faced injustice and even death—and it did not matter. They were filled with something otherworldly to achieve their mission.

The power of the Spirit ushered in Pentecost, where the disciples and three thousand others gave birth to the church. The Holy Spirit empowered them toward endurance, assurance, vision, capacity, and expertise. We need all those things and more to be effective in the hood. We have work to do, and it boggles my mind that anyone would attempt to do it without the power of the Spirit.

Christ promised that through the power of the Holy Spirit, we would accomplish even greater things than he did. He told us that it was for our good that he was going away, because if he didn't, the Spirit couldn't come.

> But very truly I tell you, it is for your good that I am going away. Unless I go away, the Advocate will not come to you; but if I go, I will send him to you. When he comes, he will prove the world to be in the wrong about sin and righteousness and judgment: about sin, because people do not believe in me; about righteousness, because I am going to the Father, where you can see me no longer; and about judgment, because the prince of this world now stands condemned. (John 16:7-11)

We can't accomplish anything that will leave a legacy without it being authorized by the Holy Spirit. So both we and the hood have hope because of what Jesus accomplished. Otherwise we would have no good news to spread. We would have no answers for the sins we face daily or the social sins we experience in the hood. This is all possible because Jesus sits at the right hand of God the Father. Because he has empowered us through the Holy Spirit, we now can change the world. If that doesn't get you excited, I don't know what will!

GUARDING OUR HEARTS

Our heart is central to our lives. In the Bible, the heart is often referred to as the place where everything is rooted. Our behaviors are only the tip of the iceberg. The truth lies beneath the surface, in the heart. So regulating our heart is the key to maintaining God's empowering presence.

I just turned fifty years old. It's amazing to me that even with half a century of living, I'm still discovering how much my heart needs to be cleansed by the Spirit. You would think I would know myself by now, and I do. But it's like I'm a book, and every year I discover a new chapter. The plot lines never stop.

We are all masters of self-deception and must work hard to stay centered in truth. The inability to do this is revealed at the root of Jesus' running conflict with the Pharisees. It's not that the Pharisees were wrong; they really did try to keep the law. Their problem was that they misunderstood the rules because they didn't know what the rules meant. In other words, their hearts weren't right. Let's examine one of the many conflicts Jesus had with them.

> At that time some Pharisees came to Jesus and said to him, "Leave this place and go somewhere else. Herod wants to kill you."
>
> He replied, "Go tell that fox, 'I will keep on driving out demons and healing people today and tomorrow, and on the third day I will reach my goal.' In any case, I must press on today and tomorrow and the next day—for surely no prophet can die outside Jerusalem!
>
> "Jerusalem, Jerusalem, you who kill the prophets and stone those sent to you, how often I have longed to gather your children together, as a hen gathers her chicks under her wings, and you were not willing. Look, your house is left to you desolate. I tell you, you will not see me again until you

say, 'Blessed is he who comes in the name of the Lord.'"
(Luke 13:31-35)

At this point in Christ's ministry, no one was interested in shielding him from risk, and certainly not the Pharisees. In fact, they were hot on his trail. They were disingenuous in their concern for his safety. Tired of him not being part of the establishment, they wanted him out of the picture. Yet Jesus was clear on his mission, and he wouldn't let anyone stop him. He was set apart by God and he was holy.

Jerusalem is not just any place. It is the Holy City. It has been set aside for God's service, and it's supposed to be a place that displays the characteristics of God. It symbolizes the center of the spiritual world. Yet it was far from its purpose. Israel rejected the prophets sent to it. The die was cast; it would continue its historical trend and reject the very one who was sent to save it. Christ wouldn't let anything distract him from his mission to die there, not even heartbreak. He is forever the model we must follow.

His life reveals to us that the journey begins within. We can't take anybody anywhere we haven't been. At the core, ministry is an expression of God's work within us. The world is broken, and one of the byproducts is the hood. How heartbroken are you? As you're reading this book, I'll assume you're willing to do something about it. The question is, Will you do it God's way, or will you let heartbreak derail you? If you minister in the hood, you will be heartbroken. Don't lose your faith over it.

Successful urban ministers master the art of interpreting their heart. They don't stand for self-deception. Three years into my church-planting experience, things were going extremely well. We had started with my family and grown. Through the wonderful generosity of our parent church, we acquired an old big-box hardware store to renovate. Through the gifts of foundations and

Christian business professionals, $350,000 was raised toward renovation. We were on our way. Or so I thought. In a six-month period, we lost a third of the congregation. There were a variety of reasons for this, but a big one was people bailing on the idea of doing church in the hood.

I was in a place of despair. Here were people I had invested in for years leaving both me and the vision. To be honest, my spirit was weak, my will failing, and I was ready to resign. But before I did, I decided to go on a fast and seek wisdom. When I emerged, it was clear that God was not calling me to quit. The Spirit was leading me to focus on chasing the kingdom. Regardless of the response of others, my job was to call them to truth and right-eousness. Those years I spent pastoring in the hood have made me the Christ follower I am today.

Are you weary in well doing? Don't ever give up. God's got you.

5

DOING HEALTHY CHURCH

SEVEN HABITS TOWARD SPIRITUAL MATURITY

WHILE RELAXING IN HIS RECLINER, a man received an unexpected phone call. He could barely hear the person on the other end, as she whispered. "I'm not talking loud because I don't want your aunt to hear me. She has Alzheimer's and doesn't want you to know. I think you need to come visit ASAP."

This revelation jarred the man, but his sense of urgency increased when he found out his aunt was the primary caretaker of her husband, who was in home hospice. To top things off, they were six hours away, and he had a full work schedule in the days ahead. But this was family, so he felt it necessary to do what he had to do. He cleared his schedule and drove down the highway, his mind abuzz with questions: How bad off were his aunt and uncle? Who oversees their personal affairs? How long is it going to take to sort these things out? He had no idea what he was going to walk into.

The man arrived and wasn't there more than five minutes when a member of his relative's church came to offer support. Then three more showed up, one with a clipboard in her hand. "Here's your schedule. I have a social worker lined up for tomorrow morning, then an appointment with an attorney in the afternoon to set up any legal paperwork. Reps from the funeral home are on their way to talk with you about your uncle."

The coming days brought a steady stream of church members offering food, comfort, and fellowship. He knew this was the fruit of the Christian lives well lived by his aunt and uncle. People couldn't help enough, and testimonies of the couple's character flowed like water from a faucet. In just three days, everything was done. Their personal affairs were arranged. And soon after the man's uncle passed away, the funeral also was set. As the man began his drive home, he was grateful.

How do I know all this? Because that man was me. I just described my first week of September 2019. So I can testify that *nothing* empowers people like a vibrant, healthy, local church. And I believe there are seven habits a healthy church congregation should focus on. These habits have been taught globally for decades and was the blueprint that I used as a church planter in the hood. That church (River of Life) will celebrate its twentieth year anniversary this year, so it's proven.[1]

It's important to note that I am presenting these as the habits that individual congregants should develop. In other words, these are the characteristics of a healthy congregation. As I stated before, the churches are people, not buildings. In part two I'll talk about the church from an institutional perspective.

Let me make a prediction. When you get done reading these habits, you're going to say, "I knew that." I believe one of the travesties of my generation is we've made church more complicated than it needs to be. Let's uncomplicate things.

HABIT 7: DISCIPLESHIP

I know you expected me to start with the first habit, but it's best to lead with the end in mind. The order of these habits demonstrates a journey toward spiritual maturity, with healthy discipleship among members being the endgame. Disciple making serves as the foundation of the other habits and runs through them all. Simply put, a disciple is one who accepts, lives out, and helps spread the teachings of another person. Therefore, a Christian disciple is a person who practices the teachings of Jesus as a lifestyle.

After his resurrection, Jesus told his disciples to go make disciples; this is known as the Great Commission (Matthew 28:19-20). It isn't optional for followers of Jesus Christ, and it's clearly what he expects the focal point of the individual Christian's life and the church's life to be.

When ministering to people in the condition of poverty, many think the goal is to get them out of it. If that's our goal, we're vastly failing as well as overestimating social mobility. Few are likely to switch social classes. *The goal is to make disciples.* Living in poverty doesn't prevent someone from becoming a mature follower of Christ. The American church must embrace the principle that, regardless of background, all people can be discipled to become faithful Christians.

Effective disciple-making flows from relationships. Churches should create pathways for young believers to be discipled, and mature Christians should be mentors. When using the term *young believers*, I'm not talking about age. I'm referring to people who are young in their expression of their faith.

Jesus demonstrated the priority of discipleship in his earthly ministry as he spent most of his time investing in a small group of young believers. He could have built a much larger public following. Indeed, his popularity grew as he performed miracles (John 6:1-15). After his resurrection, when his popularity could have reached epic proportions, he chose to spend his time teaching his disciples (John 20:19–21:25; Acts 1:1-11). The whole point of discipleship is to experience life with Christ as we do life together.

Jesus built close relationships with his disciples, and we are to do the same. We see the example in the New Testament of how Barnabas invested in Paul, who invested in Timothy. Our goal as mentors is to encourage our disciples to grow into maturity, becoming more like Christ, and then to invest themselves spiritually into another person. Being a disciple and a mentor lasts an entire lifetime.

Here are some tips that have worked in my life that may work in yours.

Find someone to disciple. Get together with a young believer, or start a group to mentor regularly, ranging from once a week to once a month. People love to meet over a meal or coffee. Initially commit to meeting for no less than ninety days and no more than a year. The point is to establish a lifestyle of personal holiness. You can use a book of your choosing, but I find that, in the beginning, the relational time spent is much more important—and most people don't (or can't) read the book. Holiness is caught more than taught.

Start with a commitment to discuss these four questions honestly. I find this quickly fills the meeting times.

+ Is there anything I need to repent of?
+ Is there anyone I need to forgive?
+ What am I grateful to God for?
+ What has God taught me lately?

Another option is to go through this chapter, laying out habits for building Christian maturity and holding each other accountable to practice them. Go through the steps slowly and carefully, so the disciple understands the meaning of each habit and begins to implement them. This can be done individually or in a group setting.

Some people will leave you and some will stay with you. Discipleship failures can be some of the most hurtful situations you experience as a Christian. Remember, even Jesus had a betrayer. And some people simply disappear before the stated timeframe is up. Remember that any disappointment is worth the risk.

You will begin to know each other so well that strengths and struggles become apparent, as people see better than they hear. This is where true growth toward Christ happens. As you move into long-term discipleship relationships, there are four primary purposes.

+ *Grow in the knowledge of the Bible.* This is when people carve out time to read books together and discuss how to apply to their lives what they learn.

+ *Let accountability for living holy lives flow naturally.* The three biggies that trip most people up—power, money, and sex—should be frequently discussed. Honesty is the best policy.

+ *Live out the other six habits.* The discipleship process is complete when those you mentor start mentoring others.

+ *Enjoy a lifelong spiritual friendship.* If you remain in a discipleship relationship for three years, you're likely to be in it for a lifetime. Both joy and pain are regularly shared, families get to know one another, and you truly do life together.

This doesn't mean that everyone in the group is at the same spiritual level; rather, it's simply a recognition of continued spiritual growth, with everyone learning from one another. These special friendships can be some of the most wonderful relationships on this earth!

Note that the frequency of meetings may decrease, and there may be no set meeting time. The meetings will be based primarily on friendship and encouragement. Following are some practical considerations.

If you're married, family comes first. Discipleship in your family should be the top priority. It starts there, *then* moves on to others. Our greatest testimony is a healthy marriage and a strong family. If you're always accessible to others outside your family, there's a problem. There will be periods when our spouse and kids need more of our time. It's important to be sensitive to their spiritual needs and development. We should seek to disciple a limited number of people outside of family at any given time.

Do discipleship in groups instead of one on one. We're limited in how many people we can invest significant time and energy in. Jesus spoke to the masses, but he invested personally in twelve. Even among the Twelve, he gave added time and attention to a special group of three: Peter, James, and John (Matthew 17:1; 26:37). A good number to consider is between one and three others. Meeting in threes (mentor and two disciples) or fours (mentor and three disciples) provides a good dynamic for learning and interaction.

Selection is critical. We can disciple only a limited number of people, so we should pray for direction. For the most part, the people Jesus selected were quite ordinary. The issue is not ability or education but teachability and a desire to grow spiritually. These two attributes are the most important to look for.

Make expectations clear. Although it isn't necessary, some mentors may ask their disciples to sign some form of agreement. I think the best place to start is short term, anywhere from at least three to no more than twelve months, with meetings ranging from weekly to monthly. Establishing expectations is especially important if crossing gender lines. For example, if working with a woman, I always had my wife sign off, and we'd meet in a public setting. If privacy was required, we met at my house with my wife present in another room.

Be flexible. These are guidelines, not rules. Effective discipleship is not just a checklist. People grow at different speeds and in different ways. Each disciple-mentor relationship is different and will have unique circumstances.

HABIT 1: REPENTANCE

The first step in becoming disciples is repentance. Repentance can be defined as the changing of mind that results in a life of surrendered obedience to Christ. Repentance is an ongoing experience in church life. Repentance doesn't maintain our salvation; rather, it's an expression of our salvation. As we grow spiritually, our lives are increasingly characterized by an awareness of sin, a desire for an intimate relationship with God, and regular confession of our sins (1 John 1:9-10). The word *salvation* reflects a move away from danger and imprisonment toward a place of safety and blessing. It also speaks of deliverance from the consequences of sin to a restored relationship with the Creator.

The challenge we face is that, in order to have a relationship with a holy God, we must be absolutely perfect, as he is. This perfection deals not just with our actions but also our attitudes.

However, we all fail to live up to such a standard. If we're honest, we agree with the Bible's assessment of the human condition: "All have sinned and fall short of the glory of God" (Romans 3:23). But the message of the gospel of Christ is the good news of salvation. So how do we move from the bad news to the good news?

The answer lies in the phrase "salvation is by grace through faith in Christ." God's grace refers to his kindness toward those who deserve punishment. It's undeserved and can't be earned (Ephesians 2:8-9). Salvation is through faith in Christ, and we receive God's grace when we have this faith. Faith embraces the ideas of belief, trust, and reliance. We all have faith in something or someone, but the vital question is, Where do we choose to put our trust (John 3:16)?

Concerning the roles of faith and repentance in salvation, some Scriptures mention faith alone as necessary for coming to Christ for salvation (John 3:16; Ephesians 2:8-9; Romans 10:9). Others refer to repentance as the condition for salvation (Luke 24:46-47; Acts 17:30; 2 Corinthians 7:10). Perhaps it's best to say that saving faith includes repentance (Mark 1:15).

As we mature in our faith, we become more tuned in to sin. It's the church's job to name it. Indeed, the closer we draw to Christ, the more we see unholiness. At salvation, our sin nature is forgiven but not removed. And, as Christians, we still sin, which disrupts our relationship with God. But as we continually repent, God continually forgives (1 John 1:9). When we repent, God wants us to confess our sins. Rather than focusing on our beautiful words or formulas, God looks at our hearts. Are we truly sorry for displeasing God? Do we care deeply about restoring our close fellowship with God? Do we ask for the Holy Spirit to help us become more like Christ?

Since repentance is the changing of one's mind, which results in a life of surrendered obedience to Christ, we are to look patiently for outward evidence of that change. Jesus called this evidence "fruit" (Luke 6:43-44). This fruit won't be perfected, because believers are all in process. But if the Holy Spirit lives within us, we will seek to obey Christ and become more like him (Galatians 5:16, 19-25).

More than a simple acceptance of spiritual truths, the faith Jesus speaks of is dependence as we surrender to him. Do you want to live life for God or for yourself? Further, has the Holy Spirit provided in your life a confidence that you are a child of God (Romans 8:14-16)? Jesus promised that when the Holy Spirit came, one of the primary roles would be to convict people of wrongdoing (John 16:8). This conviction touches our heart, head, and hands. In other words, there is a change of heart and head when the Spirit works in us, which results in changed behavior. This conviction with repentance continues all the days of our lives.

HABIT 2: PERSONAL DEVOTIONS

To practice personal devotions is to quiet ourselves and concentrate on our spiritual life. If you're like me—a doer by nature—this takes effort. Having devotions feels like I'm doing nothing, wasting my time. Yet we all need to nurture our spiritual life outside church gatherings. For this to occur, we must spend regular time alone with God. If Jesus himself had to do it, why not us (Luke 5:16; John 6:15)? Our relationship with Christ grows as we spend alone time with God, enabling us to make course corrections when needed.

Personal devotions are based on a desire and on a decision to maintain and energize our spiritual life. They are an ongoing necessity with many benefits (Psalm 51:6). When we practice them regularly, we gain wisdom and insights (James 1:5). Alone time with God releases the power of the Holy Spirit, enabling us to forsake the pursuit of the limelight, to forgive, to serve, and to be generous (Ephesians 1:17-19).

There are four essentials to practice for this to be a success.

Setting is everything. Find a quiet place that allows you to withdraw briefly from relationships and routines in order to reflect. This could be as easy as getting up early or staying up late, when you know everyone else will be asleep. Or go off into nature, if that's your thing.

Make your time God-centered. Be God-centered by focusing on studying what a passage teaches you about God's character. This helps put circumstances into perspective. If we aren't careful, our devotions turn into whine-and-moan sessions. Always understand that God is in control, and spending time in reflection reinforces this truth (Philippians 4:6-7).

Pray. Prayer can be defined in many ways: as a personal conversation with a personal God, or as talking with God and making our needs known. At its core, praying involves trusting God to hear us and answer us. It's believing God even when we lack feelings of faith or don't see the results we want. Praying is yielding ourselves to God's purposes and being willing to be a part of the plan, not making God part of our plans. Whether short or long it does not matter; just be sure to do it regularly.

Capture your experiences. While studying for my PhD in educational leadership, I learned that one of the best teaching methods is to have students journal. Keep a record of the experiences you have with God. Write, type, or even record your feelings, weaknesses, hopes, and discoveries. State any impressions God places on your mind or heart. If you are gifted in the arts, write prayers, poems, or music, or draw or paint.

HABIT 3: CORPORATE WORSHIP

As we practice repentance and personal devotions, we must also realize that we aren't meant to live the Christian life alone. Rather we are to commit to a local church and participate in corporate worship. A central idea of this book is that Jesus promised to build his church (Matthew 16:18). When we commit to a local church, we share a unique identity as the people of God. Simply put, since Jesus established the church and promised to build her, we need to value her. As the body of Christ, the local church is the representation of Jesus' life on earth.

If we miss connecting to the body of Christ, we miss Christ (Ephesians 1:22-23). As the bride of Christ, the church represents close and intimate relationships between Christ and the people redeemed. When we connect to the local church, we enjoy the privilege of knowing and fellowshipping with Christ in the most meaningful ways (Revelation 19:7).

Jesus protects the local church and cares for her. When we connect with other Christians, we receive Christ's care for us through others in the church. Likewise, when we care for others, we truly touch them with the love of Christ (Ephesians 5:29-30). Jesus demonstrated the high value of the church by voluntarily dying for it. Such sacrificial love teaches us to value and to commit to a local church regardless of its imperfections (vv. 25-27).

Corporate worship. One way we value the local church is through assembling for corporate worship. There are several priorities in corporate worship, the first being the study of Scripture. The Bible is the clearest revelation of God that we have. The early church saw unprecedented miracles and experienced the powerful arrival of the Holy Spirit. Instead of focusing on the supernatural, they "devoted themselves to the apostles' teaching" (Acts 2:42). By their behavior, they sent the message that miracles and wonders are not an end in themselves but rather are confirmation that this new message was from God. Therefore we must make the study, understanding, and application of Scripture a priority.

Early Christians lifted their voices in praise to God, as such praise was only natural (Ephesians 5:19; Acts 16:25). Sometimes a controversy over the style of music in a church arises. Whatever a local church decides, it's important to make sure that our music is biblically accurate and honoring to the Lord (Colossians 3:16-17). Additionally it's wise for the musical style not to be the main reason a believer joins a church. Although singing is important, we must also evaluate whether the church values other priorities, especially the study of Scripture.

Prayer. Both individual and corporate prayers were practiced in the New Testament. We find that prayer was an essential component in the Jerusalem church (Acts 2:42). The model for faithful prayer was Jesus, who took time away from the crowds to seek his Father and set aside special hours to commit major events to God (Luke 3:21; 6:12; 9:28; Matthew 26:36-45).

Generosity. The early church practiced this (Acts 2:44-45; 1 Corinthians 16:2). It refers not only to giving money but also to giving our time and talents.

Baptism and communion. The early believers faithfully followed Jesus' command of baptism and devoted themselves to the breaking of bread as visible reminders of the death and resurrection of Jesus (Acts 2:38; 1 Corinthians 11:23-26).

Church attendance and involvement. There are legitimate reasons for not attending church regularly, such as health issues. However, most professing Christians who choose not to attend corporate worship regularly make excuses, such as being disappointed with the hypocrisy of the people; being tired of conflict; disapproving of the preaching or style of music; feeling inconvenienced by the service schedule, and so on. Though these may be legitimate reasons, the biblical expectation is for us to attend corporate worship consistently. The New Testament is clear: there is no concept of a true Christian who is not faithfully involved in a local church (Hebrews 10:24-25). Following Christ and belonging to a church have always gone hand in hand.

HABIT 4: SMALL GROUPS

It's important for a believer to continue to grow in Christ through relationships with other Christians. One of the best ways to cultivate such relationships is in small circles of fellowship. Small groups come in various types and exist for a variety of purposes. During his earthly ministry, Jesus accomplished much of his teaching and discipleship in small-group settings, especially with the twelve disciples (Mark 3:13-14). In addition, the early church met in small groups (Acts 16:40; Romans 16:5). The following activities can take place in this setting.

+ *Regular Bible study.* I am partial to sermon-based studies, where members reflect on the previous week's sermon. This provides opportunity for each member of the group to ask questions and participate in discussions. Or a study can be done using a Christian book or specific topic.

+ *Regular prayer support.* Pray for and/or with each group member, the church, and the neighborhood.

+ *Caring.* Take time for members to practice generosity by tending to the physical needs of members or by providing encouragement in times of crisis, illness, or loss.

+ *Fellowship.* Small groups are an excellent setting for relationship-building activities that lead to friendships in a nonthreatening environment.

+ *Evangelism.* Group members intentionally building relationships with friends, relatives, neighbors, and associates in order to share the gospel.

+ *Discipleship.* Many churches use small groups as their main vehicle to practice discipleship with trained leaders.

Practically, small groups should be formed when the church attendance reaches thirty adults. Until a church has more people, the church itself should function as a small group. The minimum number of people in a small group should be five, with the maximum of around fifteen. The pastor—or key church leader— should spend time teaching the congregation about the importance of a small-group ministry. A very important principle to remember is that a small-group ministry will be only as healthy as the leadership of the small groups.

When getting started with small groups, the pastor or a key church leader is the manager of the group and trains the initial core of small-group leaders. The core should be made up of spiritually willing and growing individuals who demonstrate leadership potential. As the small-group ministry begins to expand, the pastor or key church leader trains others through on-the-job training before creating another group.

As for a meeting place, all that's needed is a comfortable place (home, church building, etc.). The meetings should last from one to two hours at least once a week and no less than twice a month. There are a variety of ways they can be composed, such as men or women only, intergenerational, age-based, etc. A simple meeting format can be meet-and-greet with light refreshments to start, Bible study, then prayer for needs.

As the small-group ministry develops, questions will arise about creating new groups or adding more people to existing groups. The church may choose to add people to existing groups regularly or to have several new small-group starting dates during each year—or a combination of both.

Groups must be a safe place for personal sharing. If the group members already know each other well, it may be valuable to add them to existing groups. If people don't know each other, it's best to add them to new groups, which should start at different times during the year.

New small-group starting points may be seasonal, and small groups may stop meeting for a few weeks between the seasons. During this time, the start of new groups may be announced. After the break, the leaders of existing groups can either continue to meet with the same group or start a new group with two or three members from their previous group. Church and small-group leaders must always invest time and effort in discipleship and in building up new leaders.

A church won't have effective new small groups without new leaders prepared to shepherd them. Periodically it's important to discuss the effectiveness of the church's small groups with its small-group leaders. Also frequently provide opportunity for testimonies and sharing to the entire church on how lives are being changed through the small-group ministry.

HABIT 5: COMMUNITY ADVOCACY

Seeking the common good is what creates a church without walls. As I stated earlier in the book, the best way to reach the hood is to seek the common good by being a compassion and justice center. It makes the local church an anchor within the community. I'll talk extensively about this in a later chapter, but for now I'll give guidance for the individual church member.

When Jesus assigned his disciples ministry tasks, he said there would be times of difficulty in their future. They would simply be following in Jesus' footsteps (Matthew 10:17-18, 24-25; Luke 9:23; John 15:18-20). So for us, it's essential to understand that faithful community advocacy isn't easy. At times, the challenges can even shake our faith. But with increasing perseverance in ministry and as we trust God, we grow stronger in faith and are better equipped to show the self-giving love of Christ (Psalm 23:4; Romans 8:28; James 1:2-5).

When a person becomes a follower of Jesus, the Holy Spirit indwells him or her. And the Holy Spirit provides each person with at least one spiritual gift and typically many (1 Corinthians 12:4-7). No one person has all the gifts. The Holy Spirit helps every Christian to love God and to love others. The Spirit convicts us of sin and of our need for repentance in order to have a right relationship with God (John 16:8-11; 1 John 1:9-10). The Holy Spirit also fills us with a loving desire to honor God in obedience (John 14:15-21; 1 John 2:3-6). It's the Spirit who gives us assurance that we are children of God (John 1:12-13; Romans 8:14-16).

The Spirit creates within us a desire to be with other followers of Jesus and to have right relationships with them (John 15:12-17; 1 John 2:9-11; 4:7-8). He also gives us hearts of compassion and justice. Gifts given by the Holy Spirit aren't to be used in a selfish manner. Rather we are to use them lovingly to glorify God and to be a blessing to others (1 Peter 4:10-11; 1 Corinthians 12:4-27). When Christians learn to use their gifts, neighborhoods change.

The New Testament contains several lists of spiritual gifts (Romans 12:6-8; 1 Corinthians 12:8-10; Ephesians 4:11; 1 Peter 4:10-11). The fact that there are several lists indicates there isn't one exact or complete list of spiritual gifts. In fact, it's likely there are many other gifts not mentioned. Pray and ask God to make your spiritual gifts clear to you.

Also examine your natural abilities. What can you do well? What are your strengths? Sometimes God blesses us with service in areas in which we are weak. But most of the time God uses our natural abilities for service. Consider your interests. What do you like doing? What are your passions? What are you interested in? Ask your friends what they think your spiritual gifts are. Use your gifts to serve the neighborhood, and see what God blesses.

HABIT 6: EVANGELISM

Each member of the Trinity is involved in evangelism. The good news about Jesus flowed from the heart of God the Father, who lovingly sent his Son to our fallen world (John 3:16). With the heart of an evangelist, Jesus sacrificed his life for the glory of God that the lost may be reconciled to God. Before Jesus left this earth, he directed his disciples to share the good news of his kingdom throughout the world. To do this effectively, they were equipped with the empowering presence of the Holy Spirit (Acts 1:8).

Since God demonstrated the priority of evangelism, we should too. Some come to Christ through a church service; others through reading the Bible; others through a healing or vision. But research has consistently demonstrated that most people become Christians through a personal relationship, typically through a family or friend.[2]

Often our family is our most important evangelistic opportunity. We must faithfully pray for our family members that they will come to a personal saving faith in Christ. We also must live our lives as a witness before them. The most powerful Christian witness to our kids is through cultivating a loving marriage. If we want them to see the truth of Christ, we must demonstrate the light and love of Christ in our marriage. If you are a parent—single or not—invest time in teaching your kids to follow the Lord. As a result, they may also bring up a new generation of faithful Christians, who will in turn touch many lives.

Beyond your family, commit to pray for the salvation of at least two non-Christian friends. These friendships may be from your childhood or may include neighbors or coworkers. If you do not have two non-Christian friends, ask God to direct you to them. Often the longer we are a Christian the fewer non-Christian friends we have. This is particularly the case for those in full-time Christian ministry, as all their time is usually spent with other Christians.

If you don't have at least two non-Christian friends to pray for, make lifestyle changes to be around more of them. Perhaps add an activity, such as having a neighbor over for dinner, get to know the parents of your children's friends, etc. Even if this means less time at church, develop some friendships with non-Christians.

Allow your evangelistic conversations with your friends to develop naturally. They shouldn't be forced, awkward, or tightly programmed with techniques. Rather look for opportunities to share the gospel within true, authentic friendships. Also connect your non-Christian friends with other believers by inviting them to special church events and activities, such as a special program, a holiday church event, or a service project.

Recognize that your non-Christian friends are especially open to the truth of Jesus during difficult times. When life-altering events occur (such as the loss of a job, a divorce, a physical illness, or the death of a loved one), they are likely struggling and exploring issues they don't usually think about. If you've developed a healthy friendship and are present during such times, your friends will be more willing to hear what you have to say.

Know that friendship evangelism may not yield quick results, though some of our non-Christian friends may surrender to Christ very quickly. Some never will submit to Christ. Leave the results to the Lord.

Repentance, personal devotions, corporate worship, small groups, community advocacy, evangelism, and discipleship—I am sure you have heard all these concepts before. The question is, Are you doing them? Are you leading others to do them? Is your church organized around these seven basic habits, or has it gotten sidetracked? There is nothing more empowering to the hood than healthy local church members, and these are the habits they practice.

PART 2

SEEKING THE COMMON GOOD

6

FAITH AND WORKS

ELIMINATING THE TENSION BETWEEN EVANGELISM AND JUSTICE

IN A SMALL TOWN there were only three churches, and they operated in great unity. The town was located at the bottom of a mountain, and it had a dangerous road that ran through it that was the cause of many fatal car accidents earning the nickname Dead Man's Curve. The churches decided to have a meeting to come up with ideas on what to do about it.

They collected enough money and volunteers to purchase an ambulance and start a rescue program. That way those injured on Dead Man's Curve could be rushed to the hospital in the neighboring town as soon as possible. The plan worked to perfection as volunteers ensured a successful operation twenty-four hours a day, seven days a week. Many lives were saved even though some people suffered injuries that would remain with them for the rest of their life.

Every Wednesday night the volunteers would have dinner together. One day a visitor attended and heard the story about the situation and the response. She was impressed yet confused at the same time. She boldly floated an idea. "Why don't you all close Dead Man's Curve and build a tunnel instead? That should pretty much solve the problem." The volunteers told her that it was possible, but it would cause an unsolvable issue. The mayor owned a restaurant and gas station that benefited from the road's customer traffic. The tunnel idea would be a nonstarter for him.

The visitor pushed back, reasoning that the mayor's economic interests should not matter more than the people who die and are injured regularly. She suggested that the pastor of the church where the mayor was a member float the tunnel idea by him. And if he wouldn't listen, maybe as a last resort organize a campaign to vote him out of office, as it would save lives.

The volunteers now felt the visitor had worn out her welcome. "We're called to spiritual matters, not politics," one of the volunteers snapped back. Another chimed in louder, "We're called to share the gospel and show compassion!" The visitor realized things were going sideways, and politely excused herself from the dinner before any more tension arose. As she left the dinner, one question gripped her soul: Is it more important to operate the ambulance to pick up the dead and injured than to try to prevent injuries in the first place?[1]

WHY THE TENSION?

We're now entering the second part of the book, which is focused on the concept of the common good. What is "the common good"? It is the answer to two questions. What do those who have put their faith in Christ have in common with those who have not? And what can the local church do to make the world a better place for them? The local church ought to understand differences and act on commonalities. God wants all neighborhoods to flourish, and they can't if institutions don't function well.

There should be no tension between evangelism and justice within the body of Christ, as it's unnecessary to prioritize one over the other. The Bible clearly does not. Both are biblical and two sides of the same coin: proclaiming and demonstrating the work and witness of God. To complete the God-ordained mission of the church, you can't have evangelism without justice. There is no fulfillment of the Great Commission without following the first and second greatest commandments to love God and to love your neighbor as yourself.

Before Jesus ascended into heaven, his last topic was evangelism. He told his followers to make disciples of all nations, and he said he would send the Holy Spirit to empower them to do so (Matthew 28:19; Acts 1:8). This was not a suggestion but a command with the expectation that their very existence depended on the success of their efforts. They weren't to be afraid, as he authorized and empowered them to perform this task.

And that task has no boundaries. They were to start where they were, which was Jerusalem. That city was also the site of God's outpouring of the Holy Spirit, which happened at Pentecost. Many of those who would first be converted would have a wide range of relationships within the city, so it makes sense to start there. However, Jerusalem also was the place where following Christ was most controversial, as he was crucified there in the not-too-distant past. So evangelism there would not go unchallenged.

Eventually persecution hit, and they moved on to the next closest target: Judea. This was an area filled with people who had a shared Jewish culture. But their culture was distinctly Judean, as it was far from Jerusalem. This area was the first target of expansion for the early church.

Samaria proved to be the most difficult part of their marching orders. Basically it was an order to go tell their enemy about Jesus. There was no love lost between the two groups. Samaritans were considered half-breeds because they were descendants of intermarriages between Jewish people and other nations. They didn't associate with one another—period. Yet Christ made it clear the Christians were to go and witness there, regardless of the historical friction.

The gospel was then to spread to the ends of the earth. Wherever they went, they were to tell people the story of Jesus. This would happen only if they multiplied themselves through discipleship. As more and more converts were won, at some point the task would be completed. Of course, we're still taking the gospel to the ends of the earth. We are to go to people we like and dislike. We are to be local and global. If we aren't, we won't be following our Lord's commands, and the church won't be healthy.

It would be good to note the content of the message that was spread. The best outline can be found in Acts 10:34-43. During this sermon, Peter preached on three points: the opportunity to experience salvation; the life, death, and resurrection of Jesus; and the call to faith considering the coming judgment. We see some other things added to this basic outline in other sermons recorded in Acts, but those three points are consistently a part of the proclamation.

That is a basic understanding of evangelism most Christians share, and it's not controversial. But things go sideways when the topic of justice comes up. You may come from a denomination or church network that's still fighting the social gospel battle. Or your church may have no idea of any tension between justice and evangelism. Regardless of where you land, if you are to minister in the hood, you need to be aware of this tension.

That tension didn't develop out of thin air. In the late nineteenth and early twentieth centuries, great change began to occur in American demographics. Chasing the lure of having a higher quality of life, people began to migrate to cities in record numbers. Immigration, industrialization, ethnic and religious diversity, and poverty brought great societal challenges. They stretched city social services to the point where they often broke down. Poverty, isolation, and alienation within cities were unintended consequences.

The church began to respond to the new world that was developing around it. Initially the primary response was advocacy based on private action and personal responsibility. Organizations such as the YMCA, YWCA, and Salvation Army were formed mainly for the purpose of urban reform. Most denominations and church networks were on board.

Another response was the social gospel movement, which began around 1880. Christians in this movement emphasized the elimination of societal sins and downplayed personal holiness. They developed a new theology based on their new emphases. They attacked historical positions, such as the Bible being the authoritative Word of God as well as the concept of the original sin of Adam and Eve. This caused a splintering into two major camps of Christian traditions: fundamentalist and progressive. That's an extremely brief synopsis of what Christian historians call the Fundamentalist-Modernist controversy. I encourage you to investigate it if you haven't yet, as I believe this historical moment is the biggest influencer of the tension we feel today.

WE SEE BETTER THAN WE HEAR

No one comes to Christ without (1) receiving a clear presentation of the gospel and (2) seeing a demonstration of what the kingdom of God is all about. We mistakenly believe that evangelism is an event, such as a "bring your friend to church" day or a crusade in a stadium. God certainly can use those. However, when we survey the Bible concerning evangelism, we see that evangelism happened organically within a web of relationships. This is more than likely how you came to know Christ.

Two things collided to bring you to Christ. The first was your circumstances, which led you to go on a spiritual journey. Some of us were at rock bottom; others felt they were fine until they wandered into a Bible study. Or you may have a testimony like mine. Being a churched kid, it never dawned on me to consider Jesus *wasn't* real.

The second thing that brought you to Christ was realizing that living the Christian life made practical sense to you on some level. And it made sense because you were convinced by a demonstration that Christ is real.

I'm evangelizing a couple right now. Both have been deeply hurt by life experiences. I sense they also may be struggling a bit in their marriage. I've already told both about Christ numerous times, as I've known them for years. Now I'm actively working to get them to my church's small group on marriage and/or a church service. I want them to see the power of people doing life together. In the meantime, I just hang out with them as often as I can to strengthen the bonds of our friendship.

Looking briefly at how the early church shared the gospel helps resolve any tension between justice and evangelism. Honestly, I don't think the early church felt any. Biblically evangelistic and justice-oriented acts apparently were carried out side by side without any thought of conflict. They experienced a radical demonstration of what the love of God looked like—faith and works that demonstrated the faith.

Look at how they naturally combined evangelism and justice at Pentecost (Acts 2:42-47). Three thousand people were saved based on Peter's preaching. The new believers were organized into home groups immediately to begin the discipleship process. Those who had enough shared generously with those who didn't. There was no theological wrangling about the rightness or wrongness of that. There was an immediate recognition of the responsibility of believers to work together so there would be no need among them.

The established order was to care for each other materially as part of their demonstration of the good news of salvation that had just been announced. God used this generosity to grow the church daily. We see this principle of community responsibility continue when issues regarding caring for widows were worked out (see Acts 6).

No one comes to Christ simply through an intellectual understanding of God. We can get many *confessions* for Christ through the preached word, but if we want *conversions*, demonstration is needed. My former professor used the hand as an illustration of the human experience. The palm represents our spiritual base; it unites the physical, mental, emotional, moral, and social aspects of our human existence. Together, all these aspects work as a portal to connect people to God.

We are much more than brains on a stick, and life is more than intellectual rationalization. Even the very act of proclaiming the Word depends on demonstration.

For people to receive the message, they must trust the messenger. If they don't deem the person to be authentic, the message has no power to convince. For the Christian, the pursuit of justice is simply part of being a credible witness who proclaims the good news of salvation to a sinful world.

Seeking justice isn't done at the expense of proclamation. The Bible is to be lived out. It can be studied and systematized, but it's more than a philosophy; it's a blueprint for life. We should never force ourselves to choose between right belief and right practice. Both are needed if the gospel is to advance. James 2:14-18 makes things clear:

> What good is it, my brothers and sisters, if someone claims to have faith but has no deeds? Can such faith save them? Suppose a brother or a sister is without clothes and daily food. If one of you says to them, "Go in peace; keep warm and well fed," but does nothing about their physical needs, what good is it? In the same way, faith by itself, if it is not accompanied by action, is dead.
>
> But someone will say, "You have faith; I have deeds." Show me your faith without deeds and I will show you my faith by my deeds.

Evangelism is much more than just the verbal exchange of ideas. That's inadequate, according to James. If we claim to follow Jesus, action that demonstrates our faith is expected. In other words, if you were accused of being a Christian in a court of law, is your lifestyle evidence enough to convict you?

There is no contradiction between the teaching of James and verses in the Bible such as Romans 3:28: "a person is justified by faith apart from the works of the law." James didn't teach that we can earn our salvation through good works; he was saying that our faith is proven to be true when we back it up with good works. The good works prove that what we say about our faith is the real deal.

After all, by saying we are Christian, we claim to have a relationship with the God of the universe. How can someone say she has such a relationship with nothing to show for it? And how can we invite someone else to have such a relationship and not *expect* them to look for proof? A verbal claim is short of being enough. The fruit of our lives is the receipt showing that we have been bought by Christ.

James was adamant about favoritism (James 2:1-4). He criticized a congregation for playing favorites toward a wealthy man over a poor man. The wealthy man was made to feel welcome and given a great seat at the gathering, while the poor man was shuffled off to a bad seat. James ushered a harsh rebuke, reminding us that the poor and the rich are equal in God's eyes. This is also what Jesus taught.

BIBLICAL JUSTICE

When many hear the word *justice*, they think payback. In our culture, justice is typically associated with punishment for a wrong that has been done. When someone is acquitted of a crime that it seems he committed, people demand justice. We're programmed this way because the American legal system is slanted toward *retributive* justice—a system of criminal justice based on the punishment of offenders rather than on rehabilitation.

However, there is another type of justice called *restorative*. We can certainly see examples of retributive justice in the Scriptures, but restorative justice is more prevalent. It has to do with restoring situations to their rightful place. Also note that, in the Bible, justice and righteousness are intertwined and are always related to people, never to things.

Justice and righteousness revolve around the fact that humans are made in God's image. *Righteousness* means what it sounds like—that is, doing right things in the middle of the wrong around you. It's the display of dignity and fairness within relationships.

Justice is a moral quality of God that we see heavily emphasized in Scripture. God is presented as the author of the idea and is committed to its enforcement. It is one of his ways of relating to the peoples of the world.

Justice united the people and the institutions of Israel through that nation's law codes. In fact, it's because of the justice of God that they remained hopeful. The Jewish faith was built on trusting in the sovereign authority of God as judge to take care of any and all situations they found themselves in. God, as a sitting judge, pronounces who is righteous, as we see many narratives of people pleading their case.

Those considered righteous live by their dedication to God's laws. This protects them from their enemies. This is in sharp contrast to those who are considered wicked. Many people and nations dig their own graves as a byproduct of their sinful injustices.

In the New Testament, the stress is on righteousness, but we must not make the mistake of thinking this is a sharp departure from justice; remember, the concepts are intertwined. Paul often used the concept of righteousness interchangeably with salvation. He also used it as a reference for how to act morally, often tying it to the justice written in the Mosaic law. We see a third and closely related use when he discusses Christian ethics.

Like evangelism, justice and righteousness play out in a web of relationships. Relationships happen on two levels. The first is personal, and the second is social. On a personal level, we've all experienced being offended. We feel we were wronged, and therefore the situation was unjust. Second, the sum of human interactions makes up a society. When groups of people experience injustices, we have a whole dictionary of terms used to describe the situation. These are nicknamed "the isms": racism, classism, sexism, ageism, and so on.

When an injustice occurs on a personal or social level, we want to work toward restorative justice, restoring relationships and making situations right. This is at the heart of the church's pursuit of justice. Just as we want reconciliation on a personal level, we want it on the societal level. On both levels, that happens when the biblical principle of respecting others as the image of God is applied.

A good portion of Old Testament teaching involves justice for the poor, with numerous passages discussing widows, orphans, prisoners, and slaves—that is, the underclass of that time. We also see concern about topics such as fair wages.

The Scriptures describe three main categories of people in poverty. First are the destitute, who are dependent on other people to make ends meet. They are the street-corner panhandlers that we see today. Second are those who have a physical ailment that causes them to live in poverty. Third are those who are psychologically defeated. Life has broken them down so much that others must support them materially. The writers of the Old Testament consistently chastise Israel for allowing people in these conditions to be exploited and oppressed.

The book of Deuteronomy is filled with political and economic regulations meant to level wealth to benefit the less fortunate. A major one was regulating the forgiveness of debt every seven years. So it's clear that Israel was expected to protect the rights of the poor and to give them pathways to escape their poverty.

However, the laws were merely there to instruct the heart. God wanted the Israelites to care about what poverty did to others. It wasn't just some religious duty to perform. It was to spur generosity and compassion for their neighbors. After all, this was a people who had experienced the worst life had to offer while serving as slaves in Egypt. God didn't want them to forget what he had delivered them from.

When we look at the writings of prophets such as Jeremiah, Isaiah, and Hosea, we gain a firm understanding of restorative justice. Many of the Old Testament writers followed a pattern of reprimanding the Israelites for their violation of God's laws and of warning the coming punishment. Yet it never stopped there. There was always a plea for them to turn from their wicked ways and turn back to God. It's made clear that God desires to love them back into relationship. We see an example in Ezekiel 16:59-63:

> This is what the Sovereign LORD says: "I will deal with you as you deserve, because you have despised my oath by breaking the covenant. Yet I will remember the covenant I made with you in the days of your youth, and I will establish an everlasting covenant with you. Then you will remember your ways and be ashamed when you receive your sisters, both those who are older than you and those who are younger. I will give them to you as daughters, but not on the basis of my covenant with you. So I will establish my covenant with you, and you will know that I am the LORD. Then, when I make atonement for you for all you have done, you will remember and be ashamed and never again open your mouth because of your humiliation, declares the Sovereign LORD."

The people of Israel had once again been unfaithful to God, breaking promises. What they deserved was retributive justice. Despite their behavior, God's promises were kept. All that was required for the covenant to be renewed was that they turn back from their wicked ways.

In chapter three, I discussed Jesus' teachings concerning the poor, so I won't repeat myself here. But I'll mention one example from the New Testament:

Jesus entered Jericho and was passing through. A man was there by the name of Zacchaeus; he was a chief tax collector and was wealthy. He wanted to see who Jesus was, but because he was short he could not see over the crowd. So he ran ahead and climbed a sycamore-fig tree to see him, since Jesus was coming that way. When Jesus reached the spot, he looked up and said to him, "Zacchaeus, come down immediately. I must stay at your house today." So he came down at once and welcomed him gladly.

All the people saw this and began to mutter, "He has gone to be the guest of a sinner." But Zacchaeus stood up and said to the Lord, "Look, Lord! Here and now I give half of my possessions to the poor, and if I have cheated anybody out of anything, I will pay back four times the amount."

Jesus said to him, "Today salvation has come to this house, because this man, too, is a son of Abraham. For the Son of Man came to seek and to save the lost." (Luke 19:1-10)

Zacchaeus was an unrighteous man who worked in a system of injustice, which was tax collecting. It would be an understatement to say both he and the system were wildly unpopular. He was considered a traitor on every level, as he cheated his people daily for the sake of the himself and the Roman invaders. Jesus went to *his* house to dine? Yes, he did, because he was about restorative justice. He wanted to make things right. Zacchaeus accepted Christ by faith and immediately began reforming the institution he worked for by paying restitution for those he cheated.

THY KINGDOM COME

Let's put evangelism and justice in the context of the Lord's Prayer. Notice that central to the prayer is the concept of God's will being done on earth the same way it is in heaven.

This, then, is how you should pray:

> "Our Father in heaven
>
> hallowed be your name,
>
> your kingdom come,
>
> your will be done,
>
>> on earth as it is in heaven.
>
> Give us today our daily bread.
>
> And forgive us our debts,
>
>> as we also have forgiven our debtors.
>
> And lead us not into temptation,
>
>> but deliver us from the evil one." (Matthew 6:9-13)

Typically heaven is viewed as a faraway place above the clouds. The first thing we need to understand about heaven is it's not as far away as we think. The universe is not set up like a cosmic three-decker parking garage with heaven on top, the earth in the middle, and hell on the ground floor. The biblical record presents the story as God making one good creation, and heaven and earth are two parallel dimensions.

I've mentioned the significance of the fall. In the first two chapters of Genesis, we read about how the earth was created. Eden is essentially heaven's backyard, as heaven and earth are joined at the hip. When we get to Genesis 3, sin enters the world, and creation is split into the two dimensions of heaven and earth. That's the state of things until Jesus comes back.

Heaven remains uncorrupted, but we all know that right now earth is very corrupted and not a great place to live. However, this is not the world our heavenly Father created. Romans 8:18-25 is very instructive concerning this. It points out that the world is broken because of sin. In this broken state, the earth is exposed to failure, oppression, and decline, which hinder God's original design. Although things look bleak around us, in the end we win. God has promised there will be a new heaven and earth that will free the world from the bondage of sin and evil. Revelation 21–22 makes it clear that creation will be restored to its original glory, where heaven and earth are sewn back together. When Christ returns, we will live on a renovated earth.

Second, the Bible presents heaven as mission control for earth. It's the cosmic universe CEO's office, the place where directives for world order are given. Jesus said in the Great Commission in Matthew 28:18, "All authority in heaven and on earth has been given to me." Scripture says repeatedly that Jesus is in heaven, ruling the whole world, and he will one day return to make that rule known to everyone. Therefore, in the prayer we are to ask that God make things on earth the way they are in heaven.

Third, heaven is not our final resting spot. When we die, we'll consciously experience the love of God the Father like we never have before. And we'll be in the presence of the Lord, so that's not too shabby. Heaven is where all that will take place, but really heaven is a cosmic waiting room. And what will we be waiting for? The same thing we were waiting for while we were on earth: the second coming of Jesus Christ. Our final resting place is earth.

What's supposed to happen in the meantime? That's what the Lord's Prayer is telling us. To fully understand this prayer, we've got to pretend we're first-century Jews living in Palestine. That was the original audience Jesus taught this prayer to. If you said "in heaven" to them, they wouldn't associate the phrase with the afterlife.

Heaven was not viewed back then as it is today, as an escape from the trials of this present world. To say "in heaven" was a reference to God's sovereign rule over all creation. We are citizens of heaven, right now, not when we die. The phrase "on earth as it is in heaven" literally means to bring heaven to earth. Our marching orders are to enter the earth's brokenness and to do our best to fix it until Christ comes back, which involves both evangelism and justice.

SALT AND LIGHT

I hope I've convinced you that evangelism and justice are connected, which can alleviate any tension. They are both vital components of our faith and help us further God's mission. Taken together, they help us be the salt and light Jesus talked about.

> You are the salt of the earth. But if the salt loses its saltiness, how can it be made salty again? It is no longer good for anything, except to be thrown out and trampled underfoot.
>
> You are the light of the world. A town built on a hill can't be hidden. Neither do people light a lamp and put it under a bowl. Instead they put it on its stand, and it gives light to everyone in the house. In the same way, let your light shine before others, that they may see your good deeds and glorify your Father in heaven. (Matthew 5:13-16)

During Jesus' time, salt was used as a preservative. That was its value, so if it lost its saltiness, it was of no value. If we sit on the sidelines and watch a sinful world go by, what good are we toward accomplishing God's mission? We've already been put in the game. Will we decide to play?

We run the risk of not being used by God, which can happen only if we become too much like the world. We should not try to fit in. We are to be countercultural to give people an opportunity to see what the kingdom of God is all about. We should lead the way toward justice and righteousness, just as good salt brings out the best taste in meat.

Similarly, if you are a city on a hill, everyone can see you—especially if that city is lit up at night. People can see that city for miles all around. That's how our lives are when we practice evangelism and justice. People can see the light of Christ when we stand for those who can't stand for themselves.

7

THERE GOES THE NEIGHBORHOOD

UNDERSTANDING THE POWERS THAT BE

EMPOWERMENT IS SOMETHING GIVEN TO US, not something we already possess. We are to live a life of action, combatting the evil around us through the gift given to us: the Holy Spirit. The roots of our struggle do not originate with other humans but with evil forces commanded by Satan. The hood is the hood because of sinful human beings and broken institutions.

I'll never forget when I spent time with a pastor from Uganda who ministered when the dictator Idi Amin ruled the country. I couldn't relate to his stories of the incredible evil he witnessed. That pure evil snuck up and *surprised* me. He told me that the difference between the two of us was that I expected things to go right in my life. Because of his experiences, he didn't have such expectations. Yet he had not lost his belief in a good God. He fully understood the power of a strong faith to combat the hell around him, regardless of the odds.

Few of us understand evil. We imagine evil as something in a horror movie. An evil character is simply the opposite of the good character, so things balance out, making for a good storyline. This can deceive us, making it seem that evil is needed for the world to function. But that is far from the biblical case. Genesis 1–2 makes it clear that the evil world we live in is *not* the world God created. And Revelation 21–22 tells us we'll get back to God's original design of an evil-free world one day.

Evil is a *real* problem with spiritual roots, so we can't treat it with kid gloves. Despite daily evidence to the contrary—mass shootings, corruption, sexual abuse, etc.—people continue to believe the world is fundamentally good; it was until Genesis 3 happened.

I have many friends who are social justice activists. They always challenge me to get more into the game. Tweet more, write more on injustice, march more. They're probably right in pushing me in that direction. However, as good friends do, I push back. I ask, Do you have a church home that you attend more Sundays than you miss? When is the last time you cleared your calendar and spent time with the Lord? Have you ever organized a prayer meeting for the community? Who's holding you accountable for living a holy life? The hood has enough humanitarian do-gooders. It doesn't need lukewarm Christians who live spiritually neutral lives.

Holiness is the way to victory because it deals with the root of poverty—evil. I'm not saying poor people are evil; the condition they live in is. Evil is the root cause of that condition. God doesn't want anyone to do without the resources necessary for a good quality of life. Therefore, we must go beyond advocacy to work toward redemption.

GIVE THE DEVIL HIS DUE

Don't ever forget we are at war. The apostle Paul wrote, "For our struggle is not against flesh and blood, but against the rulers, against the authorities, against the powers of this dark world and against the spiritual forces of evil in the heavenly realms" (Ephesians 6:12). Satan is not a cute Halloween character. Demons are more than sports mascots. The Bible says Satan stalks the earth like a roaring lion, looking to devour people (1 Peter 5:8). He has an army of demons to help accomplish this. This is not kid stuff; they are very real. Before us is a powerful enemy that has humanity in its crosshairs.

A single woman who works fifty hours a week cleaning hotel rooms can't make ends meet. Her rent keeps going up because the neighborhood she grew up in is gentrifying. Her children are struggling at the neighborhood school because that school is just horrible. Don't make the mistake of thinking that the answer to her situation doesn't have a spiritual core. Fatalism and despair dominate her world. She has little hope that she can better her situation, as her life is difficult and oppressive.

Spirituality isn't just a part of our lives but the core that binds all of life together. Again I remind you of my professor at seminary who used an illustration of a hand with each finger representing one of the five aspects of the human experience: physical, mental, moral, emotional, and social. The palm of the hand is the spiritual. It's what makes us human, serves as the essence of our existence, and it holds all the parts of our being together.

We need supernatural spiritual power to defeat the army of Satan and bring transformation to the hood. We war against invisible dark powers. Paul didn't develop a systematic theology of the dark powers. But he did mention these demonic forces enough to make it clear they are real and that the church is expected to engage them. Ephesians 6:12 describes the Christian life as a struggle against evil spiritual forces. It's also important to note that "heavenly realms" is not a reference to heaven or a mysterious space between heaven and earth. It is the reality of what the people of God have been made holy to do (see Ephesians 1:3-4).

Dark powers are manifested through social and cultural forces. Social forces affect everyday life; cultural forces are the values, attitudes, and beliefs we hold. They are intertwined, exert power, and have both a physical presence and a spiritual core. The five foundational institutions of any society (government, economics, education, religion, and family) are sociocultural creations. They are good and sinful at the same time. God created them to be a blessing, but they have been infected with evil.

Few people have a problem understanding sin and the need for personal salvation. Historically that has led to an emphasis on seeing evil strictly on an individualistic level. This approach doesn't allow for a full understanding of reality and severely limits ministry in the hood.

Scripture presents redemption as both personal and societal. To understand Christ's work of redemption, the sovereignty of God, and the value of the church, they must be emphasized in the church just as strongly as personal salvation. It's no coincidence that Christian traditions that balance all three have a strong history of engaging societal sin. Both the abolitionist and the civil rights movements were birthed from theologies that engaged the public.

Because I planted a church in a neighborhood in the middle of a race riot, I came to understand societal sin quickly. Trauma has a way of waking us up to the reality of evil. It caused me a significant amount of leadership pain, which is often the best teacher. Yet I would not trade that experience for the world. Because of it,

I understand deeply why the Bible emphasizes the need for a people of God and for the New Jerusalem. Institutional and societal sin needs to be disrupted.

Think of an institution as the total sum of choices made by individuals in relation to how to operate and design that institution to perform a task. Institutional awareness is important because institutions heavily influence all of us toward certain life choices. And they can be structured in such a way that they work actively to prevent or to enhance human flourishing. It's a mistake to think the problems of the hood can be solved strictly through philosophy, politics, education, economics, and legal advocacy. Institutional influences have spiritual cores that must be accounted for.

INSTITUTIONAL INFLUENCE

The five foundational institutions (government, economics, education, religion, and family) are connected. There is no clear border where one stops and another begins. This means there is constant interaction that results in either holiness leading toward the common good or evil leading to suffering. A major task of the church is to move institutions toward the common good, disrupting demonic control. There are several biblical examples of when God wasn't pleased with the direction of institutional influence of a city. The most obvious is the city of Jerusalem, which is mentioned many times in the Bible as sinful. Institutional power was influenced by evil to the point that the residents were suffering. Jerusalem, which means "city of peace," was not living up to its name. For example, consider this passage about Jerusalem.

The word of the LORD came to me:

"Son of man, will you judge her? Will you judge this city of bloodshed? Then confront her with all her detestable practices and say: 'This is what the Sovereign LORD says: You city that brings on herself doom by shedding blood in her midst and defiles herself by making idols, you have become guilty because of the blood you have shed and have become defiled by the idols you have made. You have brought your days to a close, and the end of your years has come. Therefore I will make you an object of scorn to the nations and a laughingstock to all the countries. Those who are near and those who are away will mock you, you infamous city, full of turmoil.

"'See how each of the princes of Israel who are in you uses his power to shed blood. In you they have treated father and mother with contempt; in you they have oppressed the foreigner and mistreated the fatherless and the widow.'" (Ezekiel 22:1-7)

Jerusalem had outdone itself. It had become disgraceful, awful, and cruel. The desire for it (and all cities) was that it reflect God's presence; instead its spirituality had become toxic. What created that evil environment? Its institutional influencers, the princes of Israel. None of them were being held accountable, so God intervened.

Officials were abusing their power, treating citizens with disrespect in order to get rich. They had gone beyond mistreatment toward inhumane oppression of the vulnerable populations of immigrants, orphans, and widows. The flow of the economy had been corrupted to the point where the morality of the transaction was not a consideration. Maybe the worst culprits were in the religious establishment.

Her priests do violence to my law and profane my holy things; they do not distinguish between the holy and the common; they teach that there is no difference between the unclean and the clean; and they shut their eyes to the keeping of my

Sabbaths, so that I am profaned among them. Her officials within her are like wolves tearing their prey; they shed blood and kill people to make unjust gain. Her prophets whitewash these deeds for them by false visions and lying divinations. They say, "This is what the Sovereign LORD says"—when the LORD has not spoken. (Ezekiel 22:26-28)

The priests didn't do the things necessary to distinguish the people of God from the rest of the pack. The prophets turned a blind eye to all the evil the institutions were committing. God called them liars. They despised holiness and made God out to be human. I don't know if worse charges could be made against those who were supposed to be God's representatives.

For Jerusalem, the result of massive institutional failure was the judgment of God. I can't go so far as to say that this is the fate for every city that reaches that level of corruption. But it's clear that corrupt institutions are not pleasing to God. It's also clear that cities themselves possess a certain spirit that isn't neutral. And religious institutions play a critical role in regulating the common good of a city.

HOODS DON'T JUST HAPPEN

Considering this discussion of institutions, it's clear that hoods don't just happen. Dark powers have utilized institutions to ensure there are haves and have-nots in every urban area. One of their most powerful tools is racial oppression.

I use the terms *race* and *ethnicity* interchangeably, though technically race is categorizing people genetically, and ethnicity is categorizing people by shared history, cultural roots, and a sense of shared identity. I do so because most people view the terms as the same thing, as it is basically impossible to categorize people accurately by biological race.[1]

So we must accept the fact that racial discrimination is an evil way of life within our foundational institutions. America's historical records suggest that we should start with the premise that race influences everything we do in society. We experience this as *racialization*.

A racialized society is a society wherein race matters profoundly in relation to life experiences, opportunities, and social relationships. It allocates different economic, political, social, and psychological rewards to groups along racial lines. Basically, racialization is the process in which one group of people imposes a racial element into a social situation, often to oppress others and/or to impose certain values and treatment.

Because we live in a racialized society, dismissing racial identity by proclaiming oneself or an institution as colorblind is common and not helpful. There is an historical template showing how institutions operate during the creation of "bad" neighborhoods. "Bad neighborhoods" typically means black or brown ones that have a high concentration of poverty. If we look at the segment of poor people living in extremely poor neighborhoods (that is, in concentrated poverty), we see how poverty has been quarantined to certain areas, mainly among nonwhites in US cities (see figure 4).[2]

Racial Disparities in Concentrated Poverty

Percentage of poor blacks and whites living in concentrated poverty, by metro area

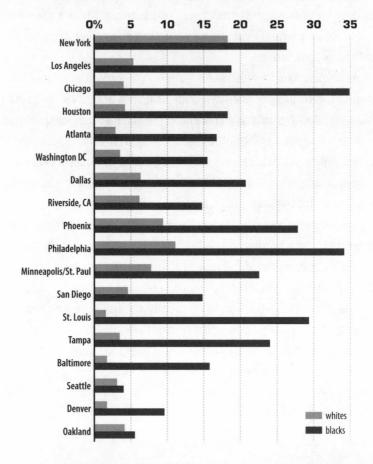

Figure 4. Racial disparities in concentrated poverty

This means that urban whites and nonwhites experience the condition of poverty very differently. It's segregated and communal; if you are poor and black, you are much more likely than a poor white person to live in a neighborhood with other poor families. This means that poverty influences pretty much everything you do (where you shop, where you go to school, etc.). Poor whites are much more spread out throughout a metropolitan area. So as figure 4 demonstrates, if we are talking about hoods, we are talking about black and brown people's neighborhoods.

Several significant factors explain how hoods happen. Most can be categorized under either violence, restrictive covenants, and urban renewal.

Racial violence. You would be hard-pressed to find an American city that doesn't have racial violence as part of its history. Major incidents have left scars that stay with us today. One of the most infamous was the Tulsa race massacre. In May 1921, a young black man, Dick Rowland, rode an elevator with a white woman. There are various accounts of what happened during the ride, but the telling of the story within the white Tulsan community escalated tension to a fever pitch, which led to Rowland's arrest.

The local newspaper's report of the event sparked a clash between black and white armed mobs at the courthouse. When shots rang out, the black group retreated to the Greenwood District, known as the Black Wall Street. On June 1, Greenwood was burned to the ground by white rioters. When the violence ended, six thousand black Tulsans had been imprisoned, thirty-five city blocks had become ruins, more than eight hundred people were injured, and an estimated three hundred were dead. Of course, not all racial violence has been this dramatic. But it's not hard to find stories of violence of varying degrees that parallel the development pattern of particular neighborhoods.

Racial restrictive covenants. Covenants became more and more common starting in 1917, after a Supreme Court ruling outlawed segregation ordinances. For example, the Civic Unity Committee of Seattle defined its covenant as "agreements entered into by a group of property owners, sub-division developers, or real estate operators in a given neighborhood, binding them not to sell, lease, rent or otherwise convoy their property to specified groups because of race, creed or color for a definite period unless all agree to the transaction."[3] In other words, where people were allowed to live could be restricted by the color of their skin. Obviously, this left most people of color with limited housing options as they were not on top of the housing food chain.

The federal government catalyzed the creation of these covenants nationwide in 1934 through the National Housing Act. The goal was to combat the Great Depression as part of the New Deal by preserving affordable housing. Hundreds of city neighborhoods across the nation were chopped up on maps, with certain neighborhoods literally outlined in red as risky investments—hence the term *redlining*.

If your neighborhood was redlined, it was nearly impossible for you to get a business loan or home mortgage. Most of the redlined neighborhoods were nonwhite neighborhoods. Banks created self-fulfilling prophecies, as the reasoning they gave for not investing was because of poor property maintenance. Any neighborhood—regardless of racial demographics—that didn't have enough capital to maintain homes and businesses would have a negative environment.

Redlining and restrictive covenants have left a long legacy. Research the history of the housing patterns of your city, and you'll see its residue decades later.

Urban renewal. Starting with the Housing Act of 1949, urban neighborhoods were targeted for renovation. The plan was to tear down the old to bring in the new. Federal funds were used to kickstart the process. By now, you know where this story is going. Nonwhite neighborhoods were targeted to be destroyed to make room for projects like the interstate system.

If your city has an interstate, it likely runs through what used to be a black or brown neighborhood. This splintered and destroyed entire communities, many of them thriving and stable before the "renewal." Many business owners and families who had been promised compensation for their property never received it.

Many other policies, practices, and procedures shape the formation of hoods. They all revolve around limiting the distribution of wealth-building vehicles to nonwhite people. At their root, they are evil institutional practices. Let these examples spark your curiosity about how the hood you minister in was formed. I bet you'll find at least one of the three at work in your community.

ADVOCACY IS NOT ENOUGH

Many times, attempts toward reformation create viscous cycles of failure. Institutions are often rigged and/or corrupt, and reformers tend to be punished. Until Christ's second coming, the world will be a sinful place. Evil will continue to exert its power over institutions to maintain the status quo.

Let me take you back to my experience of church planting in the middle of civil unrest over a racially charged police officer shooting in 2001. At that time, the neighborhood was a poor one. Since then, gentrification has hit, and I've been a keen observer of reformation efforts. Almost twenty years later, I've seen incremental progress, though it is a mixed bag concerning meaningful change within the neighborhood institutions. Some people have changed for the good. However, there is also no question that institutions have been used for evil by people in power who have utilized the trauma of the riots.

Reformation involved cleaning up the drug trade. In the early days of that church, I interacted with many who were involved in selling drugs. For some, the motivation was strictly financial. But for others, it was a grasp for power. For both groups, there was always an explanation for participation: the failing economy. In fact, among the ones I saw successfully reform, the solution was always to get them equipped to make a livable wage.

Political solutions have a way of being circular. Politicians provide solutions to problems that were created by previous politicians. Those solutions aren't motivated by the good of the people but rather by personal gain. So reforms often have unanticipated consequences, which of course require another solution.

For example, I went to meetings where the solution was to "clean up" the neighborhood through safe housing. An entity was created, backed by corporate dollars. It pretty much bought up every abandoned building. During the time I was pastoring, the neighborhood had ten thousand people living in it but a potential to house forty thousand. This of course kicked off gentrification, so now the issue is how to keep poor people from being displaced. The neighborhood is safer, but it's benefiting the original residents less and less.

My PhD is in educational leadership, so besides the church, education is the institution I'm most familiar with. I can tell you that in the state of Ohio, there is a direct correlation between poverty level and K-12 educational success. This has something to do with the intellectual aptitude of the kids but much more with the system set up to educate them.

Few are aware that our educational system is a three-way partnership. The child brings the motivation, the school provides the learning environment, and the adult guardians fill in the gaps. If any one of those factors is missing or weak, the child won't succeed academically.

Take the example of homework. What does the teacher who sends home assignments assume? That you have a healthy home environment and that you have the resources available at home to successfully complete the assignment. Neither of these can be assumed for a child in poverty. Research shows that if a kid in poverty is educated using principles applicable to the context (for example, no homework is assigned), that kid will achieve at the same rate as her richer counterparts. So the way an institution structures itself can drastically affect the lives of the people who are engaged in it.

Certainly the church should participate in advocacy efforts, while at the same time realizing we have a higher calling. Our endgame is beyond advocacy. It's the redemption of our neighborhood. How does a local church work toward that redemption? By pursuing the common good of the neighborhood.

SEEKING THE COMMON GOOD

The definitive biblical text regarding seeking the common good is Jeremiah 29, a letter to exiles. I think it's important to note who Jeremiah was. He toiled as God's mouthpiece for Judah for four decades—to no avail. He was a prophet who had no audience, as nobody listened to him. If there had been Christian conferences back then, he would not have been on the list of speakers. He also was poor and suffered many hardships.

Jeremiah was both arrested and beaten for his activity. At one point he became such a nuisance that he was deported to Egypt. His family disowned him, his neighbors rejected him, his co-workers loathed him, and he had no friends. The number-one reason his life was so hard was his calling. He was a prophet— and true prophets speak what God wants spoken, regardless of personal cost.

As far as the Israelites were concerned, Jeremiah never had anything good to say. It didn't matter to them that his message came from God. He constantly warned people of God's judgment and lamented deeply and publicly for what had become of his beloved nation. His ministry wouldn't have been considered a success by any standard that we use to judge such things. So why take advice from him? For one reason: his ministry was considered a success by God's standards, which are obedience and faithfulness.

Here's the context of Jeremiah 29: the Israelites had been conquered and exiled from Jerusalem. They were wondering what was next and how to go about their lives in their new home of Babylon. Jeremiah gave them guidance from God on how they were to proceed. The major principle he expressed was to *not* surrender to the stress and anxiety caused by the environment they were in.

He implored them to do life in the middle of the trouble. Get married, raise kids, buy a house, plant gardens, go ahead and settle in. Just because they were not in an ideal situation did not mean their lives were over. Then he gave an unexpected proclamation: "Also, seek the peace and prosperity of the city to which I have carried you into exile. Pray to the LORD for it, because if it prospers, you too will prosper" (Jeremiah 29:7).

You can see why nobody wanted to listen to Jeremiah. They had been conquered and ripped from their homeland, and he was telling them to make a home among their enemies and pray for their prosperity? Not only that, but the prosperity of the enemy was tied to their own. This is the heart of what it means to seek the common good.

But here's the tricky part, which is what separates working toward redemption from merely doing advocacy: They were ordered to do this while also remaining holy. They were to seek the common good as holy people. Remember, holiness means (1) to display the character of God and (2) to be set apart for service by God. Paradoxically, the Israelites were to be both a part of and *separate* from the community. We also can do this by understanding the differences between the church and other institutions, acting on the commonalities, and honoring the good work that's going on toward the common good outside our four walls.

NEVER FORGET YOU ARE HOLY

I once heard a story involving the late, great Pastor E. V. Hill, who was asked to give the prayer at a presidential inauguration. A White House official read the prayer beforehand and asked him to edit out the conclusion: "in Jesus' name." The official also noted that none of the other clergymen's prayers had that clause in it. Hill responded that he wouldn't agree to that, because "I plan on my prayer being heard!" This comical example gets to the crux of the argument of this book: *holiness is the way to victory.*

Jeremiah 29 makes clear that the people of God are called to work toward the well-being of the larger society. In this book, we're focusing on the hood. Actively promoting the prosperity of the neighborhood requires us to become a part of the life of the community. We should be at community meetings, become members of the local chamber of commerce, and anything else we have time for that involves neighborhood health. Why on earth would we isolate ourselves?

While pursuing the common good, we should also guard our hearts against civil religion. Sociologist Robert Bellah wrote that there are "certain common elements of religious orientation that the great majority of Americans share. . . . This public dimension is expressed in a set of beliefs, symbols, and rituals that I am calling American civil religion."[4] This religion mixes up our allegiances and way of life. It is what separates working for the redemption of a community from practicing advocacy. Advocacy is needed, but we're working for *redemption*.

While I chose Jeremiah 29 to demonstrate this, I could have used the life of Esther, Daniel, or the trio of Shadrach, Meshach, and Abednego. When push came to shove, they all chose holiness over civil religion. They lived righteously among those who weren't believers, did not trade their personal holiness for personal gain, and were used by God to influence the community they lived in. We must understand how our institutions are different from others while acting on our commonalities.

When I served as a pastor, during the aftermath of the Cincinnati riot I attended many community meetings. Some of the meetings went well; others were very nasty, with people screaming at each other, hurling insults at a rapid rate. Ironically, all these meetings had been formed to try to heal the neighborhood. Although the Black Lives Matter movement—with its alternative Back the Blue movement supporting law enforcement—was not born yet, that vibe was certainly present. Dealing with the issues our hood faced was very messy.

Like Jeremiah 29 teaches, my job was to live holy and be an agent of common good as best I knew how. Both my own and the church's creditability depended on our holiness. People may have disagreed with me and/or my religion, but they knew of my lifestyle and my church's witness of loving Jesus and the hood, and they respected that. I was a bridge builder, and like a bridge, I got walked on from both sides. To some I was a sellout; to others I was a firebrand. They were advocates for their causes, but the only thing I was an advocate for was seeking the peace of the community.

That meant getting the sides to understand each other so solutions could be found. It meant praying for everyone involved. It meant inviting both sides to come to church programming. At one picnic we had officers and the people they arrested mingling with one another. That wasn't organized on purpose; it happened because our church was respected by law enforcement and hustlers. When we threw a picnic, *all* the community showed up.

Personal and institutional redemption are the pathway toward hood transformation. They are two sides of the same coin, and it's a mistake not to focus on both. When I trained volunteers for our food pantry and afterschool ministry, I told volunteers that the people in our neighborhood need food *and* a church home; the kids need salvation *and* a high-performing neighborhood school. It was always amazing to me how people kept trying to separate the two. There is no need to do so.

8

CHAMPIONING THE COMMUNITY

EMPOWERING GRASSROOTS LEADERS AND WORKERS

AT WORLD IMPACT WE EMPOWER LEADERS in a population that few serve. Our typical program participant is bivocational and ministers at a church of fewer than fifty people with an annual budget less than fifty thousand dollars. Far too many in this situation read it as a failure. They are far from it.

Our work is reflected in our mission statement: "World Impact empowers urban leaders and partners with local churches to reach their cities with the gospel."

We have three core competencies. The first is that we are champions of the ability of the poor to own and lead ministry. The second is that we are kingdom focused, which allows for a wide range of partnerships with denominations, church and ministry networks, and local churches. And third, we have accumulated unique expertise from doing holistic ministry among the urban poor for close to fifty years.

We believe the local church is the foundational element for personal life and community transformation. Our ministry training programs are designed to be affordable, accessible, and affirming of a call to ministry, utilizing the train-the-trainer model. We value building relationships, adding resources, and offering space for renewal to assist urban church leaders in accomplishing their ministry visions.

Our short-term goal is that urban church leaders receive effective training for ministry among the poor. Within five years, we hope these churches and leaders are self-supporting, self-sustaining, and self-multiplying. Over the long term, we desire to see these ends achieved in as many cities as possible.

Throughout this book, I've shared about my time as an urban church planter and pastor in a community of poverty. That journey began in earnest in August 1998, two years before the church was planted. That month I walked into the office of the former president of Circle Urban Ministries of Chicago, the late, great Glen Kehrein.

At that stage in my life, I viciously attacked the motives of anybody in authority. I had my reasons. I was fresh off an intense episode of church abuse. For three years I had served my heart out for a leader, only to realize that the leader was manipulating me for personal gain. When it became apparent the manipulation no longer could happen, I was unceremoniously dumped, and my wife's and my reputations were smeared throughout the community.

After that, Glen mentored me for a thirteen-year period, focusing on what it means to be an effective urban minister. From him I learned that effectiveness has both personal and social components. Maybe the most important lesson he taught me was how to handle life when it comes undone. He gave me a living theology of brokenness as I watched him handle one family and ministry crisis after another with grace, dignity, and truth. He was a role model for all to follow, as I saw many who preached and taught in the public sphere about social justice but didn't work very hard at personal holiness. There's something inauthentic about operating like that.

Glen taught me that seeking the common good means correcting misuses of culture, power, and ethics within the body of Christ and our society, and working for the fair treatment of all, regardless of their social status. He helped me see repairing a broken world as an opportunity to advance the kingdom.

A big deal is often made about Ephesians 2:8-9 stressing the implications of the "not by works" phrase. Instead Glen celebrated Ephesians 2:10, stressing the importance of operating in the good works we are created to do. The message was not to be so heavenly minded that we are no earthly good.

One of the most important things Glen did for me was introduce me to John Perkins, who founded the Christian Community Development Association (CCDA). Glen was a founding member of the organization, and Circle Urban hosted one of CCDA's first national conferences. They share the same philosophy as World Impact of championing the ability of the poor. And they often use this Chinese proverb to describe themselves:

> Go to the people,
> live among them,
> learn from them,
> love them.
> Start with what they know,

build on what they have:

but of the best leaders, when their task is done,

the people will remark, "We have done it ourselves."

This chapter is an introduction to the eight key components of CCDA's philosophy, which I think are critical to reaching the hood. Originally there were the three Rs (relocation, reconciliation, and redistribution) developed by John Perkins, and over the years other concepts were added.

Relocation. One of the original components of the philosophy of CCDA, this is based on the incarnational ministry of Jesus Christ. Just as Christ relocated from heaven to take residence on earth, the thought is we are to follow this example and relocate into the poor communities we minister in. The point is to do life together with those we are called to minister among.

I've heard Dr. Perkins speak many times, and he is fond of saying things like "Jesus didn't commute back and forth to heaven." If this is the case, shouldn't the most effective ministers among the poor be those who live among them? It ties together the quality of life of both minister and congregant.

A church that follows this philosophy will often have a congregation made up of three types of people. *Relocators* are people who were not native to the neighborhood but moved in. *Returners* are people who grew up in the neighborhood, left, but chose to return. And *remainers* are people who are native and never left in the first place.

There is no question living in the neighborhood raises common good understanding to a whole new level. For example, if the pastor's kids go to the same school as the kids in the youth group, quality of education takes on a whole new meaning. Or if the pastor lives in a neighborhood that is a food desert, lobbying city hall for a grocery store becomes personal. The rationale is if the problems of poor people and poor neighborhoods are the same as the pastor's, it serves as more of an incentive to make the hood a better place.

It's been my experience that this is maybe the most controversial of the principles. The debate revolves around the question, Does effectiveness among the poor really depend on living next door? And if too many people relocate, couldn't it turn into gentrification? Not to mention the family stressors that come with living in the hood. Reality is, if the pastor (and family) are always accessible, it oftentimes leads to burnout as well as unhealthy family dynamics.

I believe at its core, the principle of relocation means relocating *our relationships*. I differ in thinking that everyone serving in the neighborhood must physically live there. There are legitimate reasons to live in or outside of it, and if a person follows this principle there are healthy and unhealthy ways to go about it. If you decide to live incarnationally with the poor, consult more Christian Community Development Association resources at www.ccda.org.

Reconciliation. One of the main jobs of the church is to teach people how to live out reconciliation. We are to engage the brokenness we find on a personal and societal level. Under the power of the Holy Spirit, we are to bring hope.

Another of the three original principles, reconciliation is seen as the heart of the gospel message. The concept can be summed up by saying love God and love people. Second Corinthians 5:17 tells us that when we become saved, we become brand new people. That is what the Holy Spirit does to us and is much deeper than behavior modification—we are a totally new creation.

The result is a redefinition of our relationship with the world around us. Maybe the best definition of reconciliation I have seen comes from the Duke Center for Reconciliation:

Reconciliation is God's initiative, restoring a broken world to God's intentions by reconciling "to himself all things" through Christ (Colossians 1:20): the relationship between people and God, between people, and with God's created earth. Christians participate with God by being transformed into ambassadors of reconciliation.[1]

The first focus is the vertical relationship of people coming to a saving faith. This happens best within a church fellowship, for reasons I laid out in the first half of the book. Meeting people's physical needs like food, clothing, and shelter is done as an act of evangelism. There is no tension between evangelism and justice.

The second focus is connecting people across the many divides that exist, particularly racial and economic. John Perkins (who is African American) served as a pastor in Mississippi among other places. He had many harsh experiences with whites, including one in which he was beaten so badly by a white police officer that he almost died.

He believed his ability to overcome his hatred for whites is an expression of his faith, and overcoming racial and social class barriers should be a mark of the gospel. We ought to model Matthew 6:10, "Your kingdom come, your will be done, on earth as it is in heaven." Instead of being the most segregated hour, churches should reflect what heaven looks like.

Meeting the felt need of those in poverty is a key. Felt need is following Christ's model of meeting people where they are. As we do this, real relationships develop over time. Because of historical distrust, meeting people where they are is one of the most effective methods we have to show our true motives. It gives space for the Holy Spirt to move in mighty ways.

Redistribution. This is the last of CCDA's original principles. To redistribute simply means to share (see Deuteronomy 15;

Leviticus 25; Acts 2, 4; and 2 Corinthians 8:13-15). Another term that conveys this is generosity. This should be a natural expression of Christian and church life.

As discussed under reconciliation, we have been made new people. Part of our newness is redefining our relationship with money and material goods. We take a different view of our possessions, realizing all of them belong to God, and we are to act as managers instead of owners.

Seeking the common good is empowerment, which is the point of Christian community development. When we live with our neighbors (relocation) and engage brokenness both personally and institutionally (reconciliation), the desired result is a redistribution of resources to raise the quality of life for all involved.

Let me reacquaint you with the concept of justice. Biblically, *restorative* justice is more prevalent. As I explained in chapter six, this has to do with restoring situations to their rightful place. Justice and righteousness are intertwined and are always related to people. Part of achieving this type of justice is to redistribute resources.

I recently had a conversation with a good friend. He invests in a group of men that I jokingly call the eternal basketball team. That's because around twenty years ago he started a team for kids in the hood. Years later they are grown men and he is still their coach, yet not for basketball but for life.

He is well off and has a fund strictly for them. Over the years, he has paid for vocational training, provided zero interest loans for them to buy cars, and even served as an angel investor for one who started a business. If they are trying to make a better life, he's there to help.

I cofounded a full scholarship program at a local Christian university for kids in the hood who maybe would not have gone to college otherwise. These were not the kids every university fought over. Rather, these were kids who had the academic potential but because of context they didn't reach their full academic potential in high school. Now, many of them are graduates and productive members of society because of the school's generosity. This is what redistribution looks like.

Church based. The entirety of this book stands on this principle that the best way to pursue the common good is using the local church as the foundation.

Listening to the community. This principle is foreign to a lot of people. Rare is the occasion that the people or organization with the power and resources lay those down in order to follow the instruction of those without resources. I can't count how many meetings I've been in when decisions concerning what was best for poor neighborhoods and its residents were made without any of the residents there.

I am always the fly in the ointment and raise the issue. I use an illustration of someone going on vacation. While they are gone, I go over to their house without their permission and renovate the whole thing. Then, when the inevitable happens and they come back angry, I say, "Just be grateful for what I've done."

Outsiders + resources − community input = paternalism. The message is "you're not qualified to make your own decisions." There is no other way to put it. This principle celebrates the gifts and talents of the residents, treating them as equals. Level of wealth should not equal level of respect.

The felt need concept revolves around the ability to hear the ideas of those who have the most vested interest in seeing the common good of the neighborhood and assisting with the implementation of those ideas. It's trusting that most of the time, they know what is best for both them and the neighborhood.

A great tool to utilize to hear the community is asset-based community development (ABCD).[2] Developed by John Kretzmann and

John McKnight, it puts the people who are usually at the margins of the community at the center. Its premise is every time a person uses his or her capacity, it empowers the individual and makes for a stronger community.

Utilizing this process unearths the desires of the residents. Holding something like a town hall does wonders for learning what the people really think is important. It also builds allies and keeps down ministry duplication.

For instance, say your church has an idea to start a food pantry to feed the poor. You utilize the ABCD process and discover there are already many food pantries in your area. Then when you hold a town hall, you find out that those food pantries only serve a certain population, but the working poor have nowhere to go for assistance. They make too much money to use the other pantries but not enough to fully feed their family. The solution becomes to open a food pantry that serves the working poor.

The process I just described is what I did when I pastored. We discovered there were a lot of neighborhood residents who had enough money for three weeks of groceries, but it was the fourth week that made things tough. The residents would use our pantry once a month, and some even volunteered to serve. It was a win-win for all.

Empowerment. I've said it earlier in this book and I'll say it again here. Our present paradigm of urban ministry is flawed, as it looks at those on the margins of society as goodwill projects instead of as people who need the good news of Jesus Christ. Poverty is seen as their identity, not a condition they live in.

Oftentimes this attitude leads to methods of helping that end up hurting in the long run. If we're not careful, ministry just becomes another form of dependency. If that happens, we don't separate the church from being a social service agency. It's like the old saying,

"Give a person a fish, you feed them for a day; teach a person to fish, you feed them for a lifetime." If someone is going to rise out of poverty, it will be because they were empowered to do so.

Consider the teaching we see in the Old Testament concerning empowerment of the poor. First, we are to provide an opportunity for individuals to improve their quality of life. Second, the persons should show intentionality toward improvement if they are physically and mentally capable. Third, when the first two happen, dignity is given to the person.

In Deuteronomy 24 and Leviticus 19, we see empowerment of the poor modeled. When it was harvest time, landowners were instructed to have their fields harvested once. What was left behind was to be for enterprising poor people to come and collect.

Empowerment is not a buzzword but a critical principle to embrace. According to the Center for the Study of Global Christianity, 81 percent of the world's Christians live on less than one hundred dollars a day. If we are serious about having healthy churches, we must be serious about empowerment.

By emphasizing discipleship through the local church and advocating for the common good, we lay the foundation to empower people. We address both systemic injustice and our sinful natures. By doing so, people transform their lives and communities.

Empowerment is a marathon, not a sprint. Maybe the most common mistake I see is people thinking that short-term initiatives will make long-term impact. There is no magic bullet; community and individual transformation involve lifelong investment and commitment.

A holistic approach. The principle expressed here has to do with not focusing on just one aspect of a person's existence, thinking it will solve everything. This is where the tension arises between evangelism and discipleship. It's not that people need salvation *or* their material needs met; rather they need both to experience all that God intended for them.

We can't oversimplify needs because people are not simple creatures. It would be cruel to tell someone who needs quality housing that everything will be all right if they believe in Jesus. Again, why does there need to be a choice?

This is where being open to partnering with others comes in. Networking is key. It usually requires more than one person or organization to meet the needs of the people in the neighborhood. Neither you nor your church will have all the answers. It's good to be able to direct people to resources to help them succeed.

Leadership development. You may have heard the phrase "work yourself out of a job." This means that we are not called to eternal leadership. I frame this principle in the form of a question, Who is your bus person? What I mean is if you are a leader and you get run over by a bus tomorrow, is there someone you have prepared to take your place?

In our era we are facing a tremendous problem. The most important ingredient for Christian community development is leadership. Yet most ministries do not have an intentional process to grow leaders. Solid leadership within an urban ministry organization is critical for sustainability.

In John 15, Jesus makes it clear that ministry fruit matters to God. The fruit of our lives is directly related to the gifting God has given us and the "work that he prepared in advance for us to do" (Ephesians 2:10). Seeing the reality of this fruit ripen is directly related to how intentionally we live our lives considering our God-given gifting and priorities. Therefore, leadership development is a high priority.

It is also important to note that level of wealth has no bearing on ability to lead. It has everything to do with learning ability, teachability, and character. If those three things are in place, the person can be molded into a leader.

Poor communities need homegrown leaders now more than ever. To develop them, resources need to be made affordable and accessible to them, And the best training is on the job. There is nothing like involving people's heads, hearts, and hands.

We should always be looking to develop, empower, and release up-and-coming leaders. Leadership development was simple in the Scriptures. There was nothing particularly special about the twelve apostles. This is an indication that leaders are developed more than naturally born. Jesus had a simple method:

1. I do, you watch.

2. I do, you assist.

3. You do, I assist.

4. You do, I watch.

And the context was relationship. He gave them constant feedback on how they were doing. He also spent more time with those who had more potential than others. He spoke with the masses, spent concentrated time with the twelve apostles, then spent even more time with three of them (Peter, James, and John).

Many invest heavily in the kids in the community. They cast a vision for them early on to get credentialed then come back and be a leader in the neighborhood. They attempt to redefine success from escaping the hood to lifting it up to make it a better place. Like all the other principles, it takes a long-term approach.

CHAMPIONS IN ACTION

Churches are assets to poor neighborhoods that are often overlooked. Those churches' members are some of the most committed volunteers of any organization. When a congregation is mobilized by a skilled leader, it becomes a neighborhood asset. Besides internal church commitment to things such as worship attendance, congregants get involved in the community through volunteering, giving financial resources, and community organizing.[3] People trained through our World Impact programs are my heroes. Their churches are models of "church without walls."

We've done research on how involved some of our participants are in reaching their community, and following are some great stories from that research.[4]

Economic development. Mike told us about the opportunities his church has developed by renting space to tenants, adding, "Now their partnership with us has been with use of that building we have on the corner. They pay rent for using it." By renting their space to other organizations, Mike's church has been able to establish partnerships with local nonprofits.

A pastor from the Midwest described how he has encouraged congregants to invest in local businesses, stressing the importance of their viability. "We did a cash mob. . . . We do prayer walks through the neighborhood, and through one of those, we met the owner of a beauty supply store. It's one of the oldest African American–owned beauty supply stores in the country."

Public safety. One of the ways church leaders add to local public safety is by practicing the ministry of presence. Several leaders spoke of ways in which their churches' presence adds to public safety in the community. Isaiah described his church's outlook as "want[ing] to be known as a safe place for people that don't have anywhere to go. That's my goal. Our tagline is 'one neighborhood connected to Christ.'" Sara described a memorable exchange in which police officers appeared at an outreach event she was overseeing for homeless people. She apologized to the officers because there were cars blocking traffic. The officer responded, "Don't worry about it. We come here and just want to thank you for all you do, for the ministry!"

Education. Although most of the churches World Impact serves are small, they are adept at making a difference through educational partnerships. One pastor explained his church's partnership with an organization that provides classes for parents this way: "Yeah, this is a program that has been designed by, I think, a government agency, [and it's] on how to teach and train and nurture children from infancy. We have a couple of parents who come, and we're hoping that we can reach a little broader." Teri described her involvement with an afterschool program for refugees. And one leader in the Midwest talked about a parenting program run by an atheist that his church was involved with.

Housing. Getting involved in housing in a major way requires significant resources. While most churches won't be able to develop housing programs, they certainly can deal with individuals most affected by lack of housing. They are clearly doing this work as a church body. Churches contributed in a variety of ways to the well-being of the environment, with most of them engaging in the improvement of their immediate surroundings. Greg stated, "We have a community cleanup once every month." His congregation is not only helping to improve its local environment but also inviting neighbors to join with them.

Justice. Leaders described a variety of ways they're involved in justice work, sometimes as churches and sometimes through individual church members. Justin said his church "created a small food pantry, because we have a small building, and the interesting relationship is our partner in that sells bail bonds." Their local ministry helps prisoners' families, who they meet through the bail bonds business next door to the church. Some church leaders have key positions in their communities that allow them to advocate about issues of retributive justice, and this often carries over into the church.

Craig mentioned one of his teammates, who works on the Human Relations Commission for their city. She reviews complaints about sexual and racial discrimination. She also served on the mayor's campaign team. Her work opens the door for other church members to volunteer at the city and to advocate for justice.

Health. Some leaders indicate various ways in which they're involved in health initiatives in their community. Most of these churches aren't involved in formal health care programs but are engaged informally in health care actions. Robert stated, "Once a month we do the pregnancy center, we do our own food bank, and then we provide coffee for them." The pregnancy center he is referring to is a mobile clinic they help run periodically through their church.

Various leaders pointed to times when their hospitality to people with a variety of mental health needs provided opportunities to engage in issues of wellness. Jeff described a young man who visits his church: "He has really bad PTSD and anxiety. He's been in some bad situations, been shot six times. And so for him to even go to what we would consider a small church of sixty to seventy-five people—that is just so intimidating for him. But to come over to his friend's house and have church on Saturday evening and have dinner and then just sing some songs and read some Scripture and share the communion . . . he's faithful."

Evangelism. Church planters point to a variety of ways in which they engage in forms of evangelism within their communities. Considering that evangelism is a holistic endeavor, much of the work previously described can be considered evangelistic. Yet some work involves more direct invitations to follow Jesus Christ.

Ricardo discussed some of the initiatives he is currently most enthusiastic about:

> I'm starting another church plant in my city, but I'm working with this believer that has been a believer longer than I have. He's filled with the Holy Spirit. We started doing outreaches in various communities. And this one community that we got to, we ended up staying. I got rid of my Harley-Davidson. I traded it for five lots in that area where we were doing the outreach. And we're going to start a tent church there.

Leaders like Ricardo demonstrate a passion for sharing a christocentric message throughout their regions and beyond. They are community champions.

9

CHASING WILD DREAMS

EXAMPLES OF FAITH, HOPE, AND LOVE IN ACTION

W HEN I SHARE THE VISION of the uncommon church, one of the frequent questions I get goes along the lines of, Which leads, serving the common good or a healthy church? Many feel they are called to community development ventures but not necessarily local church ministry. There is the real puzzle of passion, ministry fit, resources, and how these things all fit together.

If you haven't figured it out by now, I am a churchman at heart. I wholeheartedly believe in Matthew 16:18, so if there must be a choice between starting a community development nonprofit or a church, to me it's a no brainer—start a church. I've seen the following scenario play out numerous times over the years.

People get a vision to start a community development operation. It goes remarkably well. After a few years of doing it, they notice something. Within all the needs they are discovering and meeting, they learn that what these people really need (and desire) more than anything physical is spiritual guidance. At this point they add something like a small group Bible study or chapel time, and now they have just become a competitor to the churches around them. And not a very good one.

It's like drinking Coke and Diet Coke. One is the real thing, the other is an imitation. Bible studies and chapel times aren't going to cut it. The people need more than that. If you are going to lead with addressing the common good through community development, if you're successful on any level, *you will need what a healthy church provides.* Too many times, the good works and goodwill activities of community development become the tail that wags the dog of the good news of the gospel.

The philosophy I recommend is that both church and community development should be present simultaneously and work interdependently. If you have it, pursue your calling to start a community development operation and don't masquerade as a pastor. Realize from the beginning that for maximum effectiveness you will need to team up with either a neighborhood church or eager church planter. You need each other.

It's also important to note that if you go toward urban church planting, it should be considered an art more than a science. Determining a church planter's effectiveness is more like judging what makes a painting or song great than like solving a physics problem. Beauty is in the eye of the beholder.[1]

When I first started out as a church planter, I was wild. I planted my church before sophisticated church-planting methods were mainstream. Those methods wouldn't be applicable to me and my hood anyway. I relied on the old-school ingenuity that I was trained in—that is, a group of us would go out and do street witnessing, and whoever confessed Christ that week would get picked and taken to a fellowship Bible study that Sunday.

One time I went to pick up a young man I had been mentoring for quite some time, but I couldn't find him. His friends told me that he was in the car of the neighborhood drug dealer, parked across the street. I was so driven by the fact that it appeared he was going back to his old ways, I marched right over to the car and banged on the driver's-side tinted window. It rolled down, and smoke billowed out as an incredulous drug dealer stared at me. I told him my church member had to come out of there. Note: I would not recommend that form of evangelism!

I was also a dreamer. To be successful, you must be. You need a dream that attracts and inspires people. And upon achieving that dream, your little corner of the world will be changed. We would walk the neighborhood, pray, and literally put anointing oil on abandoned buildings. "What do you see in this building?" I would ask. If the person said, "an abandoned building," I wasn't interested in talking with him. But if he said something like "an after-school center," we'd dream about how to make it happen.

The biggest lesson I learned from my urban pastoral experience was that people deeply desire to live with purpose and make a difference. There were good and bad days when I pastored. But at the end of the day, when I gave an opportunity to have people dream with me, most took it. And off we went on a wild ride. No one knew where it was going but God. And that's the way it should be, as dreams should be God-sized—that is, you need God to show up to make it happen. Something birthed in our souls from the Holy Spirit can drastically change the trajectories of lives and neighborhoods. Once I read of a church that trained evangelists and pastors in rural India but discovered that their sole mode of transportation (bikes) was terrible. They dreamed of building a bike that would be tough and could navigate bad roads well. A challenge to their congregation resulted in thirty thousand dollars raised in one day. Thousands of bikes are now traversing India for the sake of Jesus. And the church ended up starting a company that built the bikes.

According to the study "The Great Opportunity: The American Church in 2050," the next thirty years will offer the greatest missions opportunity in the history of America due to the biggest and quickest numerical shift in religious affiliation that has ever happened. Church planting in the United States will need to double or triple to address population growth and the anticipated closures of older congregations. The American church needs to plant more than 215,000 churches in the next thirty years to maintain the status quo. Meeting the needs of the unaffiliated will require an additional sixty thousand churches.[2]

That is God-sized dreaming. It will happen only if God shows up and transforms the way we think about church planting, particularly in the hood. We'll never get there if we use the current paradigm, which is currently too expensive and relies too much on professional clergy. I'm a product of that system, as I was backed by a wealthy church to start my church plant, and I have degrees from both a Bible college and a seminary. I'm grateful for these things. But because I'm a product of them, I realize that system won't spark viral church planting. Vibrant churches will be planted and great works will continue to be done using our present-day system, but to go viral and to reach the heights that "The Great Opportunity" challenges us to will require new ways of doing things. World Impact has a wild dream. How can we spark the planting of 3,500 urban churches in a five-year span? At the time of this book writing, we don't know yet, but we are on a mission to figure it out.

Most think the most effective urban ministries are compassionate in nature, such as food pantries, tutoring, and community development. As mentioned earlier in the book, such activities build a platform of goodwill, which in turn provides an opportunity to share the gospel. But few ask what happens next. Say the goodwill opportunities and evangelism are so successful that it's possible to plant a church. What follows? Hopefully a vibrant church that is self-supporting, self-sustaining, and multiplying.

HIDDEN HEROES

I started this book with a quote from F. Scott Fitzgerald: "Show me a hero, and I'll write you a tragedy." I'll now edit it and make it my own: "Show me a hero, and I'll write you a tragedy—unless the Holy Spirit shows up!" World Impact has a dream of a healthy church for every community of poverty. We have a vision of transforming communities together. By together, we mean partnering with denominations, church and ministry networks, and local churches to get the job done.

We have the privilege of serving gifted pastors who nobody has heard of. Those we work with are not typically invited to be conference speakers or write books. They have full-time ministries, often with part-time pay.

When I was prepping for ministry in the hood, a seasoned ministry vet told me that it would be like plowing concrete. "But always remember," he concluded, "concrete can be plowed."

The issues urban poverty raises make this one of the most unique mission fields in the world. Urban pastors are merely following their call, the marching orders they sense they have been given by God. In fact, for many of them the call is all they have. They have no money, no training, just the sense that this is what God wants them to do. World Impact's role is to affirm their calling as best we can.

As much as possible, I put myself "in the field" so I never forget who we exist for. Let me tell you a few of these heroes' stories.

They have worship services in some of the most creative spots. I can remember one time seeing the setup of what can only be described as a flophouse. The housing was the common good piece of the equation, as most of these folks could not find housing any place else. The lobby which doubled for the worship space would hold about forty people. The pastor had no money but had a calling and had been trained by us to plant urban churches. He worked in the maintenance department for the building. The congregation consisted of the residents, who were addicted, homeless, and formerly incarcerated. This wasn't sheep stealing from the other churches in the area! It was as if Matthew 22:8-11 had come to life.

Laura[3] is a pastor we trained whose church is in the section of Los Angeles known as Skid Row. You know when you've arrived there when you see blocks of tents. This sight is somewhat surreal when set against the backdrop of skyscrapers and mountains. Her congregation is certainly a unique one.

The fact that this group gathers weekly for worship was a common good in and of itself. Yet every service starts with a meal. Many have mental illness, which is more than likely why they live on Skid Row. Laura plays the role of the consummate host, meeting and greeting each one of them. It's clear she knows them well, saying each one of their names as she embraces them. Her church is an expression of one who was once blind but now can see.

An immigrant, she came to the United States like so many others seeking a better life. However, that pursuit took a wrong turn when she ended up in jail. It was behind bars where she met Christ. She imitated the woman at the well and began ministering to the other prisoners around her as well as enrolling in our church-based seminary program site we had at the prison.

Upon release, she started the church at Skid Row. She is bi-vocational, serving as an accountant during the work week. Not many people will ever know what she is doing—but Jesus does.

When Paco, a self-proclaimed "working meth addict," first met Pastor Lance, no one could have foreseen the plans God had for him. Pastor Lance invited him to be part of a new church he was starting. Paco was skeptical but curious. He attended a few times, and when he was absent, Pastor Lance would pause the service and go get him before resuming.

Paco thought that God would want nothing to do with him because of the reckless life he lived, but the reckless love of God was stronger than his doubts and fears. Paco gave his life to Christ and started off on a new trajectory. Pastor Lance discipled him for several years.

The time came for Pastor Lance to leave to enter foreign missions, and he wanted Paco to take over pastoring the church. For the next year, Pastor Lance continued to disciple Paco, giving him on-the-job training for his new position. By God's grace, Paco was a quick study.

When Pastor Lance transitioned into the overseas mission field, World Impact missionaries joined the process of supporting Paco. They introduced him to our church-based seminary program, where he received theological training and graduated in 2007.

Paco and his wife saved money to buy a home in the same neighborhood as their church. They were able to move their meeting space from an open carport to a room set aside in their home as a house church. Through their witness, seventy-five family members and friends have become believers.

Every year their church hosts an outreach where Paco boldly and confidently proclaims the gospel. He shares his story and testifies, "If God can change me, he can change anyone."

Recently Paco began leading a local pastors' association to foster fellowship and partnership with other local churches. He bought a used travel trailer and is in the process of converting it into several portable showers to meet a need for the homeless. No doubt, he will also share the gospel that has changed his life forever.

LAY HEROES

Besides pastors like Paco, urban congregants are also my heroes. My wife, Caroline, is a therapist by trade, and often I pick up concepts from her. One of them is the acronym HALT: hungry, angry, lonely, and tired. We make bad decisions in either one or a combination of those states of being. Maybe the most common threat among urban dwellers is T, tired.

I belong to a small urban church. One of my good friends there is Donnie. We met a few years ago, and he works in the service industry. Through friendship, he and his family eventually started attending the church. A turning point in his faith was when he attended our men's retreat, like the ones World Impact does. During one of the sessions, we went off in sets of three and shared our hearts. I remember sitting with Donnie and watching him cry, pouring out his heart about his mindset at the time. He was *tired*. Tired of working at what seemed to be a dead-end job for meager earnings. Tired of being estranged from his dad. Tired of his then live-in girlfriend pressuring him to get married. Really just tired of his situation in life. After baring his soul, he expressed sincere gratitude to be able to get away for a few days with his Christian brothers for a time of renewal.

This past Sunday my wife had to tap me on the shoulder to hustle up to make our lunch appointment, because I was lingering too long in the church foyer. What was I doing? Hanging out with Donnie and his wife. (He got married!) He was informing me of his new job, and we were celebrating the journey he had taken since he had poured out his heart at that retreat. His test had become a testimony.

As with Elijah, God rarely communicates loudly; it's in the whisper of calmness (1 Kings 19:9-12). I'm convinced that's when we hear best. Donnie's life was renewed because he was given the opportunity to "Be still and know that I am God" (Psalm 46:10) and because he became a part of a local church in the hood. Hundreds of Donnies and Donnas are renewed every year in small urban churches like the one I attend.

I could go on, but you get the point. Let me be clear that I'm not concluding with these stories of people in the hood overcoming deficits for you to value them. I'm telling these stories because these are my heroes. Megachurch pastors are fine, and bookselling preachers are influential. *But these women and men in the hood are my heroes.*

I'll let others do the job of uplifting the big names; I'm here for the underdogs. They are demonstrations of what God can do when we're obedient to treat the hood not as a place of good works advocacy but rather as a stage to find out what God is doing and join in. Poverty is a condition, not an identity. Understand this and get to work.

10

THE KINGDOM IS IN US

Start by doing what is necessary;
then do what's possible; and suddenly
you are doing the impossible.

ANONYMOUS

ONE EASTER MORNING BEFORE SERVICE, I went on a walk through the hood. I ran across two young men waiting at the bus stop to go to work. With the energy that Easter brings, I wished them a happy holiday and struck up a conversation. Turns out they had no idea why I was so happy.

"It's Easter!" I proclaimed. They looked at each other with puzzled looks.

"What's *that?*" one of them asked. Now Cincinnati isn't the Bible belt, but it certainly is the Bible belt buckle. I thought they were joking. I proceeded to explain Easter to them.

His buddy shook his head like he understood.

"Yeah, okay, I know about that. We do eat a big meal at grandma's house. But I didn't know it was *religious.*" I left shaken, as I came face to face with a reality.

Many in the hood no longer think the church is relevant. Things used to be different. There was a time when somebody at some point would have took those young men to church. Nowadays that is the wrong assumption to make. Christianity has been regulated to a tradition, not a lifestyle to consider.

We are in a time when there are too many that do not find relevance in following Christ. They live in rebellion from their maker because Christians too often are so heavenly minded, they are no earthly good. Our faith is seen as cute and cuddly but not real. The only way it becomes real is if someone proclaims and demonstrates the gospel to them.

The teachings of Jesus in Matthew 25 are all to stress the principle of preparedness to his disciples. The message is that no one knows the day he'll come back, so stay ready. He tells four parables to demonstrate this point, and one of them we have already discussed earlier in the book, the final judgment (Matthew 25:31-26). He ties readiness to how we treat those in poverty. Here I'll stress another parable, which is the parable of the talents (Matthew 25:14-30).

In this story, the owner gave his workers resources with instructions to multiply them. The resources were not equally distributed, as he gave an amount to them that corresponded to their ability. This was done in order to not overwhelm them. It was a setup for each worker to claim victory. If they tried, something good would happen because the owner sponsored it.

Two of the workers put forth effort and brought the owner a return on investment. They were praised. The one not praised is the one who decided to not put forth *any* effort. He had one job (which was to try) and he squandered it.

It's not too hard to connect the dots here. God has given all of us resources, and some have more than others. And we should not think of resources strictly in the form of money—think of our time, talent, and treasure. God has given these for us to make this world a better place.

May I dare say that the only way you can fail is to not try? Most who minister to those in the condition of poverty will pastor small congregations and lead small community development efforts to transform the hood toward the common good. *That is okay.* We'll take the few talents God has given us and make a difference, and God will be pleased. Yet some of you will discover you have five talents and will be shocked by what God does through you.

In the 1970s when our founder (Dr. Keith Phillips) was a college student, God inspired him to start Bible clubs for poor kids within the inner city of Los Angeles. His vision spread, and clubs were launched in a second city, Wichita, Kansas. Throughout the decade, thousands of volunteers worked alongside paid staff, and the ministry became national.

In the 1980s the ministry expanded from kids' Bible clubs to holistic discipleship of entire families. Their needs led to starting Christian community development initiatives such as elementary schools, medical facilities, and campgrounds aimed at serving the common good of the neighborhood residents.

In the 1990s, a natural progression led to expansion into church planting, as the vast majority of those we served were unchurched. Dr. Don Davis launched The Urban Ministry Institute (TUMI) to bring seminary-quality education to those who live in urban neighborhoods. We began partnering with denominations and church networks to spark church planting and leadership development outside of our ministry.

In the 2000s, Dr. Phillips pivoted, casting a vision of World Impact missionaries being repurposed from leading ministry to resourcing grassroots community church leaders. Dr. Efrem Smith followed Dr. Phillips and advanced this vision even further, leading us into a new age of expansion. We went from exclusively serving the United States to providing global ministry training, as those trained locally took their learning home to their countries of origin.

Today as I lead as the third president, we focus on one thing. According to the Center for the Study of Global Christianity, only 5 percent of the world's pastors are trained. World Impact wants to change the world by working to solve this problem. We empower urban leaders and partner with local churches to reach their cities with the gospel. We have a dream for every community of poverty to have a healthy church. Make it so, Lord.

ACKNOWLEDGMENTS

THIS BOOK IS THE RESULT OF A TEAM EFFORT. I would like to acknowledge those who play a huge role in my life.

First, I thank my life partner, my wife, Caroline. For your love and support to me and our daughters, words cannot express my appreciation. And I thank Hannah and Gabby, who are fine young women who have brought me so much joy.

I want to acknowledge the support and love of my parents. Alvin (Sr.) and Jessie, you provided a life for me that you never had yourselves.

Next, I offer heartfelt thanks to my executive team at World Impact. For Lisa's intuition, Don's wisdom, Chip's course-setting, Daren's steadiness, and George's insights. You all bring out the best in me. And much love to my executive assistant, Karen.

For all the churches who invested in me throughout my life: Hosack Street Baptist Church (Columbus); Cincinnati Bibleway Church; Rock of Our Salvation (Chicago); Hope Evangelical Free Church (Mason); and certainly my "third child," River of Life. My heart is with you forever.

Last but certainly not least, I thank my Lord and Savior Jesus Christ. Without him, none of this is possible.

NOTES

1 ADVOCACY IS NOT ENOUGH

[1]Howard Thurman, *Jesus and the Disinherited* (Boston, MA: Beacon Press, 1996), 21.

[2]Emerson, M. and C. Smith, *Divided by Faith: Evangelical Religion and the Problem of Race in America* (New York: Oxford University Press, 2000), 7.

[3]If interested in exploring more about the situation at that time, check out Tony Carnes, "Cincinnati: Lost Common Cause," *Christianity Today*, July 9, 2001, www.christianitytoday.com/ct/2001/july8/7.15.html?share=.

2 WHAT WOULD JESUS DO? POVERTY IS A CONDITION, NOT AN IDENTITY

[1]This paragraph and the one that follows first appeared on the World Impact blog: Alvin Sanders, "How to Empower the Poor," April 21, 2017, https://worldimpact.org/blog/post/how-to-empower-the-poor.

[2]24/7 Wall St. reviewed 2017 American Community Data from the US Census Bureau to identify eleven distinct groups of Americans who are more likely than their peers to live in poverty. All of the data of this section is a summary of Michael B. Sauter, "Faces of Poverty: What Racial, Social Groups Are More Likely to Experience It," *USA Today*, October 10, 2018, www.usatoday.com/story/money/economy/2018/10/10/faces-poverty-social-racial-factors/37977173/.

[3]Some content in this section is from Alvin Sanders, *Bridging the Diversity Gap: Leading Toward God's Multi-Ethnic Kingdom* (Fisher, IN: Wesleyan Publishing House, 2013). All rights reserved. Used by permission.

3 JESUS DID, NOT JESUS WOULD: JESUS AND THE CONDITION OF POVERTY

[1]This story is adapted from Heinrich Böll's 1963 short story "Anekdote zur Senkung der Arbeitsmoral," which has been given an American twist over the years.

[2]For more facts like these, check out the World Christian Database website: https://worldchristiandatabase.org/.

[3]The story of Bob also appears in Alvin Sanders, "A Theology of Enough," World Impact (blog), November 7, 2016, https://worldimpact.org/blog/post/a -theology-of-enough.

4 THE PEOPLE OF GOD: GOD'S PLAN FOR A BROKEN WORLD

[1]Some content in this section is excerpted from Alvin Sanders, *Bridging the Diversity Gap: Leading Toward God's Multi-Ethnic Kingdom* (Fisher, IN: Wesleyan Publishing House, 2013). All rights reserved. Used by permission.

5 DOING HEALTHY CHURCH: SEVEN HABITS TOWARD SPIRITUAL MATURITY

[1]The philosophy of this chapter is based on *Seven Steps of Christian Living*, lessons by Burnham Ministries International, 2014. All rights reserved. Used by permission.

[2]See Ed Stetzer, "Why A Simple Invitation Has Strategic Power for Evangelism," ChurchPlants.com, accessed May 4, 2020, https://churchplants.com /articles/7208-ed-stetzer-why-a-simple-invitation-has-strategic-power-for -evangelism.html.

6 FAITH *AND* WORKS: ELIMINATING THE TENSION BETWEEN EVANGELISM AND JUSTICE

[1]This is a paraphrase of a story told by Ronald J. Sider in *Rich Christians in an Age of Hunger* (Downers Grove, IL: InterVarsity Press, 1977), 203.

7 THERE GOES THE NEIGHBORHOOD: UNDERSTANDING THE POWERS THAT BE

[1]It is important to note I am speaking about race, not ethnicity. These are two different concepts that space will not allow me to delve deeply into. There are many good resources that talk about the concept of race, and I recommend one that was done some time ago called *Race: The Power of an Illusion*. There are clips on YouTube.

[2]Figure 4 is based on data from Paul A. Jargowsky, *The Architecture of Segregation: Civil Unrest, the Concentration of Poverty, and Public Policy*, The Century Foundation issue brief, August 9, 2015, Appendix B, 5, https://production-tcf.imgix.net /app/uploads/2015/08/07182514/Jargowsky_ArchitectureofSegregation-11.pdf.

[3]Katharine I. Grant Pankey, "Restrictive Covenants in Seattle: A Case Study in Race Relations," 1947, University of Washington Libraries, Special Collections, Civic Unity Committee collection, box 17, folder 19.

[4]Robert Bellah, "Civil Religion in America," 1967, www.robertbellah.com /articles_5.htm.

8 CHAMPIONING THE COMMUNITY: EMPOWERING GRASSROOTS LEADERS AND WORKERS

[1]Definition taken from *Reconciliation as the Mission of God: Christian Witness in a World of Destructive Conflicts*. This was a 2005 paper from 47 Christian leaders from across the world produced by the Duke Center for Reconciliation. https://divinity.duke.edu/sites/divinity.duke.edu/files/documents/cfr/reconciliaton -as-the-mission-of-god.pdf.

[2]For more information, check out the ABCD Institute of DePaul University, https://resources.depaul.edu/abcd-institute/Pages/default.aspx.

[3]To learn more, see Studying Congregations, "Resources Frame," studying-congregations.org/resources-frame.

[4]All the names used in these stories are pseudonyms.

9 CHASING WILD DREAMS: EXAMPLES OF FAITH, HOPE, AND LOVE IN ACTION

[1]World Impact has done research on effective urban church planting. Go here to download this free resource: https://worldimpact.org/blog/post/effective -urban-church-planting. Or email me at president@worldimpact.org and we will send you a hard copy.

[2]To learn more see "The Great Opportunity," www.greatopportunity.org/.

[3]In all the stories in this chapter, names have been changed.

ABOUT WORLD IMPACT

WHO IS WORLD IMPACT?

World Impact empowers urban leaders and partners with local churches to reach their cities with the gospel—extending the truth, love, grace, and justice of God in the city.

We believe that the best way to change our world is to declare the hope of the gospel in our cities. The best way to declare that hope is to partner with denominations, networks, and local church leaders. And the best way to partner with them is through relationships.

Our roots go back fifty years to evangelistic kids' clubs—from Los Angeles's Watts neighborhood to Wichita, Kansas, and beyond. As the children we reached grew up, we saw the need for urban churches and the empowerment of church leaders to continue to transform their communities from within.

WHY WORLD IMPACT?

According to the Center for the Study of Global Christianity, only 5 percent of the world's church leaders are trained for ministry. Everything at World Impact is focused on training and equipping church leaders—making resources *affordable* and *accessible* to as many as possible. We exist to serve people who minister in communities of poverty—affirming their call and vocation. They are the transforming agents in their community.

HOW IS WORLD IMPACT UNIQUE?

World Impact is perfectly positioned to train urban church leaders.
It champions the ability of the urban poor to own and lead ministry. We believe in the power of community insiders.

World Impact is kingdom focused. By focusing on the great
Christian traditions rather than on denominational differences,
we attract a wide range of like-minded partners.

World Impact is trusted. Our decades of experience in urban
America bring partners to the table—and donors trust us to get
resources in the hands of those who need it.

World Impact is global because we are local. Given the increasingly global nature of our country, if we train leaders in major US
cities, many will take that training back to their home country,
families, and friends.

World Impact has leverage. Our staff is impacting even more
leaders by being trainers of trainers.

WORLD IMPACT'S FIVE PROGRAMS

+ *Church-based seminary.* The Urban Ministry Institute
  (TUMI) equips and resources urban leaders. It provides affordable and accessible seminary training for men and
  women in the urban context.

+ *Urban church planting.* The Evangel School of Urban Church
  Planting trains, equips, encourages, and enables Christian
  workers to plant healthy, reproducing churches among the
  urban poor. This training is designed specifically to equip
  teams to reach underresourced communities.

+ *Trauma Healing.* Trauma Healing training equips urban
  ministry workers and leaders to facilitate and host Scripture-
  based healing groups. Some participants choose to become

trained to lead their own healing groups—virally expanding their ministry.

+ *Prison ministry.* Through our Onesimus Project, World Impact trains local urban church workers and leaders toward success in discipling those who have been incarcerated. We also offer church-based seminary for those who are behind bars.

+ *Retreats.* World Impact believes in resourcing urban leaders through concise, practical, and hands-on training at women's and men's retreats.

For more information, visit our website at worldimpact.org.

C|C CHRISTIAN COMMUNITY
D|A DEVELOPMENT ASSOCIATION

The Christian Community Development Association (CCDA) is a network of Christians committed to engaging with people and communities in the process of transformation. For over twenty-five years, CCDA has aimed to inspire, train, and connect Christians who seek to bear witness to the kingdom of God by reclaiming and restoring under-resourced communities. CCDA walks alongside local practitioners and partners as they live out Christian Community Development (CCD) by loving their neighbors.

CCDA was founded in 1989 under the leadership of Dr. John Perkins and several other key leaders who are engaged in the work of Christian Community Development still today. Since then, practitioners and partners engaged in the work of the kingdom have taken ownership of the movement. Our diverse membership and the breadth of the CCDA family are integral to realizing the vision of restored communities.

The CCDA National Conference was birthed as an annual opportunity for practitioners and partners engaged in CCD to gather, sharing best practices and seeking encouragement, inspiration, and connection to other like-minded Christ-followers, committed to ministry in difficult places. For four days, the CCDA family, coming from across the country and around the world, is reunited around a common vision and heart.

Additionally, the CCDA Institute serves as the educational and training arm of the association, offering workshops and trainings in the philosophy of CCD. We have created a space for diverse groups of leaders to be steeped in the heart of CCD and forge lifelong friendships over the course of two years through CCDA's Leadership Cohort.

CCDA has a long-standing commitment to the confrontation of injustice. Our advocacy and organizing is rooted in Jesus' compassion and commitment to kingdom justice. While we recognize there are many injustices to be fought, as an association we are strategically working on issues of immigration, mass incarceration, and education reform.

To learn more, visit www.ccda.org/ivp

Titles from CCDA

Church Forsaken
978-0-8308-4555-2

Brown Church
978-0-8308-5285-7

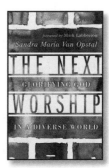

The Next Worship
978-0-8308-4129-5

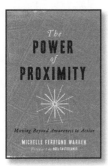

**The Power of
Proximity**
978-0-8308-4390-9

**Rethinking
Incarceration**
978-0-8308-4529-3

**Seeing Jesus in
East Harlem**
978-0-8308-4149-3

**Welcoming Justice
(expanded edition)**
978-0-8308-3479-2

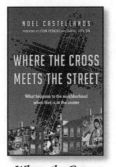

**Where the Cross
Meets the Street**
978-0-8308-3691-8

White Awake
978-0-8308-4393-0

Missio Alliance
and
≈ InterVarsity Press

Missio Alliance has arisen in response to the shared voice of pastors and ministry leaders from across the landscape of North American Christianity for a new "space" of togetherness and reflection amid the issues and challenges facing the church in our day. We are united by a desire for a fresh expression of evangelical faith, one significantly informed by the global evangelical family. Lausanne's Cape Town Commitment, "A Confession of Faith and a Call to Action," provides an excellent guidepost for our ethos and aims.

In partnership with InterVarsity Press, we are pleased to offer a line of resources authored by a diverse range of theological practitioners. The resources in this series are selected based on the important way in which they address and embody these values, and thus, the unique contribution they offer in equipping Christian leaders for fuller and more faithful participation in God's mission.

Available Titles

The Church as Movement by JR Woodward and Dan White Jr., 978-0-8308-4133-2

Emboldened by Tara Beth Leach, 978-0-8308-4524-8

Embrace by Leroy Barber, 978-0-8308-4471-5

Faithful Presence by David E. Fitch, 978-0-8308-4127-1

God Is Stranger by Krish Kandiah, 978-0-8308-4532-3

Paradoxology by Krish Kandiah, 978-0-8308-4504-0

Redeeming Sex by Debra Hirsch, 978-0-8308-3639-0

Rediscipling the White Church by David W. Swanson, 978-0-8308-4597-2

Seven Practices for the Church on Mission by David E. Fitch, 978-0-8308-4142-4

A Sojourner's Truth by Natasha Sistrunk Robinson, 978-0-8308-4552-1

What Does It Mean to Be Welcoming? by Travis Collins, 978-0-8308-4144-8

White Awake by Daniel Hill, 978-0-8308-4393-0

missioalliance.org | twitter.com/missioalliance | facebook.com/missioalliance